hamlyn
QuickCook

hamlyn

QuickCook
Hot & Spicy

Recipes by Sunil Vijayakar

Every dish, three ways – you choose!
30 minutes | 20 minutes | 10 minutes

An Hachette UK Company
www.hachette.co.uk

First published in Great Britain in 2012 by Hamlyn,
a division of Octopus Publishing Group Ltd
Endeavour House, 189 Shaftesbury Avenue
London WC2H 8JY
www.octopusbooks.co.uk

ISBN 978-0-600-62391-5

A CIP catalogue record for this book is available from the British Library

Printed and bound in China

10 9 8 7 6 5 4 3 2 1

Both metric and imperial measurements are given for the recipes. Use one set of
measures only, not a mixture of both.

Standard level spoon measurements are used in all recipes
1 tablespoon = 15 ml
1 teaspoon = 5 ml

Ovens should be preheated to the specified temperature. If using a fan-assisted oven,
follow the manufacturer's instructions for adjusting the time and temperature. Grills
should also be preheated.

This book includes dishes made with nuts and nut derivatives. It is advisable for
those with known allergic reactions to nuts and nut derivatives and those who may
be potentially vulnerable to these allergies, such as pregnant and nursing mothers,
invalids, the elderly, babies and children, to avoid dishes made with nuts and nut oils.

It is also prudent to check the labels of preprepared ingredients for the possible
inclusion of nut derivatives.

The Department of Health advises that eggs should not be consumed raw. This book
contains some dishes made with raw or lightly cooked eggs. It is prudent for more
vulnerable people such as pregnant and nursing mothers, invalids, the elderly, babies
and young children to avoid uncooked or lightly cooked dishes made with eggs.

Contents

Introduction

30 20 10 – Quick, Quicker, Quickest
This book offers a new and flexible approach to meal-planning for busy cooks, letting you choose the recipe option that best fits the time you have available. Inside you will find 360 dishes that will inspire and motivate you to get cooking every day of the year. All the recipes take a maximum of 30 minutes to cook. Some take as little as 20 minutes and, amazingly, many take only 10 minutes. With a bit of preparation, you can easily try out one new recipe from this book each night and slowly you will be able to build a wide and exciting portfolio of recipes to suit your needs.

How Does it Work?
Every recipe in the QuickCook series can be cooked one of three ways – a 30-minute version, a 20-minute version or a super-quick and easy 10-minute version. At the beginning of each chapter you'll find recipes listed by time. Choose a dish based on how much time you have and turn to that page.

You'll find the main recipe in the middle of the page accompanied by a beautiful photograph, as well as two time-variation recipes below.

If you enjoy your chosen dish, why not go back and cook the other time-variation options at a later date? So if you liked the 20-minute Spicy Vietnamese Chicken, but only have 10 minutes to spare this time around, you'll find a way to cook a similar dish on the same theme using cheat ingredients or clever shortcuts.

If you love the ingredients and flavours of the 10-minute Spiced Crayfish and Rocket Sandwiches, why not try something more substantial, like the 20-minute Crayfish, Vegetable and Coconut Stir-Fry, or be inspired to make a more elaborate version, like the Caribbean Crayfish and Coconut Curry? Alternatively, browse through all 360 delicious recipes, find something that catches your eye – then cook the version that fits your time frame.

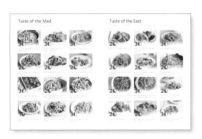

Or, for easy inspiration, turn to the gallery on pages 12–19 to get instant ideas for cooking for different occasions, for diverse flavours and palates, from the fearlessly fiery to family favourites.

QuickCook online

To make life even easier, you can use the special code on each recipe page to email yourself a recipe card for printing, or email a text-only shopping list to your phone.

 HOT-FISH-MYL

QuickCook Hot & Spicy

Spices are essential culinary ingredients, used in every nation's cuisine to stimulate the appetite and titillate the palate. Prized for centuries, they led to trade routes that spanned the globe.

Today we can create and sample exotic spiced dishes with diverse flavours, colours and textures from all over the world, in our kitchens. From the islands of the Caribbean, to South East Asia, China, India, Mexico, South America and even Africa, 'hot and spicy' conjures delightful and varied cuisines at every turn.

In this book we have recipes from all over the globe, that use spices to the best advantage, and are both quick and easy to cook. With this book, and a few essential ingredients, you can cook up a storm in the kitchen, to share with family and friends.

Fresh Aromatics and Wet Spices

Chillies: In general, green chillies are less hot and more 'earthy', while red chillies are hotter and fiery. If you want a chilli flavour with less heat, remove the pith and seeds, before chopping.

Curry Leaves: These highly aromatic leaves are used fresh in Indian and South East Asian cooking. Fresh curry leaves freeze very well and can be used straight from the freezer.

Coriander: Often the delicate leaves are used to flavour dishes, but stalks are also used, especially in Thai curry pastes.

Ginger: Fresh root ginger is peeled before using. It has a fresh, peppery flavour and is used in both savoury and sweet recipes.

Kaffir Lime Leaves: These highly aromatic leaves are usually finely shredded when using in a curry or sometimes left whole. They freeze well and can be used straight from the freezer.

Lemon Grass: This green grass is used for its citrus flavour. It can be used by bruising the base of the stalk or else chopped.

Thai Basil: Found in Oriental greengrocers, this delicate herb is used as a garnish. You can substitute regular basil if necessary.

Shallots: These small, sweet and pungent onions are widely used in South East Asian cooking. The easiest way to peel them is to slice them in half and remove the outer skin.

Store Cupboard: Dry Spices and Ingredients

Cardamom: This spice is usually used whole, in its pod, as an aromatic. You can also use the little black seeds inside the pods, by crushing them and using as part of a spice mixture.

Chilli: Whole dried red chillies add the fiery heat to a curry. Dried chilli flakes tend to have a milder flavour and chilli powders made from dried chillies vary in heat.

Cinnamon: This sweet and warming aromatic spice is available as sticks or rolled bark, and in ground powder form.

Cloves: These aromatic dried buds can be used whole or ground.

Coconut Milk and Coconut Cream: Widely used in Asian cuisine, these are added to curries to give a rich, creamy texture.

Coriander: These small, pale brown seeds are available whole or ground, and form the base of many curry pastes and mixes.

Crispy Fried Onions: These can be bought from any good oriental green grocer or supermarket. To make from scratch, gently fry thinly sliced onions in a large frying pan with a little oil, over a low heat for 15-20 minutes or until golden and caramelized. Drain on kitchen paper until crisp and dried.

Cumin: Essential in Asian, Mexican and Middle Eastern cooking, these small brown elongated seeds are used whole or ground and have a warm, pungent aroma. Whole seeds may be dry-roasted and sprinkled over a curry or dish just before serving.

Fennel Seeds: These small, pale green seeds have a subtle aniseed flavour and are used in some spice mixtures.

Fenugreek Seeds: These square, shiny yellow seeds are used widely in pickles spice mixes for curries.

Fish Sauce: Also widely known as nam pla, this sauce is one of the main ingredients in Thai cooking and a is made from the liquid extracted from salted, fermented fish.

Garam Masala: Usually added to a dish at the end of cooking time. A classic mix comprises of ground cardamom, cloves, cumin, peppercorns, cinnamon and nutmeg.

Gram Flour: Also known as besan, this pale yellow flour, made from dried chickpeas, is used widely for thickening and binding as well as the main ingredient in savoury batters.

Mustard Seeds: Black, brown and yellow, these tiny round seeds are widely used as a flavouring and are usually fried in oil until they 'pop' to impart a mellow, nutty flavour.

Nigella Seeds: Also known as black onion seeds or kalonji, these tiny matt black, oval shaped seeds are most frequently used to flavour breads and pickles.

Palm Sugar: Known as jaggery in India, this is the sugar produced from the sap of various types of palm. Sold in cakes or cans, it has a deep, caramel flavour and is light brown in colour. Used in curries to balance the spices.

Saffron: These deep-orange strands are the dried stamens from a special crocus and are use to impart a musky fragrance and golden colour to rice dishes and desserts.

Shrimp Paste: Also known as kapee, this is a pungent preserve used in Asian cooking, made from pounding shrimp with salt and leaving it to decompose. It is sold in small jars and has a very powerful aroma that disappears when cooked.

Star Anise: A flower-shaped collection of pods. Dark brown in colour, this spice has a decidedly aniseed flavour.

Tamarind Paste: Used as a souring agent in curries, the paste from this pod is widely available and can be used straight from the jar. You can also buy it in semi-dried pulp form, which needs to be soaked in warm water and strained before use.

Turmeric: This bright orange-yellow rhizome has a warm, musky flavour and used in small quantities to flavour lentil and rice dishes. It is widely available as a dried, ground powder.

White Poppy Seeds: These tiny white poppy seeds are used in Indian cooking, mainly to thicken sauces and curries.

Essential Equipment

Cooking these hot and spicy recipes does not need any expensive or complicated equipment. Most of what you will need is part of those basic essentials that every kitchen usually has: ladles, spoons, sieves, colanders, chopping boards, knives, etc. However, these essential items will help you to prepare each meal with ease.

Blender or Mini Food Processor: These are invaluable for making a smooth, well blended mixture with ease when you have to grind or combine wet and dry spices.

Electric Coffee Grinder: Excellent for grinding dry spices, they are available widely and are inexpensive to buy.

Frying Pans: Having a selection of different sized frying pans, preferably good, nonstick ones, makes light work of cooking.

Heat diffuser: This is a disc made from perforated metal, usually with a removeable handle, that sits on top of the heat source. When the pan is placed over it, it provides an even, low, well-distributed heat, perfect for slow-cook recipes and rice dishes. They are available from any good kitchen shop and are very inexpensive and will last for years.

Heavy-Based Saucepans: Having a heavy base ensures that the food cooked will be heated evenly, without burning or sticking to the base of the pan. This is especially useful when cooking ingredients or sauces for a longer period.

Mortar and Pestle: A mortar and pestle is the traditional method of combing ground spices or pastes together and is always reliable, but does involve quite a lot of elbow grease.

Wok: Essential for fast stir-fries and other dishes.

Recipes to Impress

For the perfect hassle-free dinner party

Spicy Chicken, Apricot and Cranberry Couscous 40

Rose Harissa and Chicken Meatball Tagine 54

Spicy Mango and Duck Salad 56

African Curried Beef and Mango Chutney Bake 76

Lamb Chops with Spicy Chickpeas and Spinach 88

Beef and Mixed Peppercorn Stroganoff 94

Spicy Lamb and Vegetable Stew 112

Griddled Piri Piri Squid with Mint and Coriander 140

Coconut Spiced Clams 154

Creamy Spiced Lobster Tail 156

Mustard and Curry Leaf Halibut 162

Scallop Molee 166

Lighter Bites

Guilt-free food that tastes great

Green Chicken Skewers with Cucumber and Chilli Dip 24

Piquant Chicken and Mixed Pepper Brochettes 36

Chicken, Prawn and Lemon Grass Cakes 64

Spicy Beef Koftas with Mint Relish 96

Spicy Beef Enchilada Wraps 104

Chorizo, Spinach and Egg Salad with Paprika Croutons 106

Thai Pork Larb Salad 118

Spicy Herb and Coconut Salmon Parcels 128

Tandoori King Prawn Skewers with Mint and Yogurt Dip 148

Spiced Crayfish and Rocket Sandwiches 152

Island-Spiced Sweetcorn with Avocado and Tomato 188

Cumin Potatoes with Pomegranate Seeds 194

Taste of the Med

Warm, sunny flavours from Spain and beyond

Chicken, Lemon and Tarragon Risotto 26

Spanish Turkey Stew with Lemon and Chilli 38

Spicy Ham and Pea Risotto 108

Spicy Sausage and Tomato Pasta 110

Chilli Spaghetti Vongole 130

Lemon Sole with Spicy Salsa 138

Spanish Potatoes with Spicy Tomatoes 224

Spicy Green Bean, Potato and Pesto Linguine 238

Spicy Smoked Salmon and Asparagus Pasta 244

Spicy Bean and Mixed Pepper Salad 252

Spicy Tuna, Tomato and Olive Pasta 262

Chilli and Butternut Squash Risotto 272

Taste of the East

Exotic dishes from the Orient, from China to Vietnam, Singapore to Thailand

Spicy Vietnamese Chicken 44

Thai Green Coconut-Stuffed Chicken 50

Thai Fish Ball Curry 150

Chinese-Style Runner Beans with Chilli 206

Spicy Tofu with Pak Choi and Spring Onions 220

Malaysian Red Pepper and Cabbage Stir-Fry 222

Warm Soya Bean, Ginger, Chilli and Noodle Salad 232

Vietnamese Herby Chicken Rice with Nuoc Cham Sauce 234

Spicy Prawn and Vegetable Noodles 236

Singapore Rice Noodles 256

Spiced Prawn, Coconut and Banh Pho Pot 260

Burmese Coconut Chicken and Rice Noodle Curry 276

Completely Chilli

Warm, comforting dishes that never fail to satisfy

Spicy Chicken and Mango Noodles 34

Burmese Lemon Grass and Chilli Pork 80

Spicy Chilli Dogs 98

Veal and Spring Onion Skewers with Sweet Chilli Dip 116

Chilli and Coriander Crab Cakes 134

Garlicky Chilli and Tomato Prawns 168

Sumac, Chilli and Lemon-Spiced Monkfish Skewers 170

Turmeric Mackerel Skewers with Chilli Rice Noodles 174

Aubergine, Tomato and Chilli Curry 180

Chilli, Cherry Tomato and Goats' Cheese Tart 182

Spiced Broad Bean and Dill Pilau 268

Chilli and Courgette Pennette 270

Hot, Hot, Hot

For fearless diners, these recipes really pack a punch

Thai Red Duck Curry 48

Haddock, Tomato and Tamarind Fish Curry 136

Spicy Monkfish and Mixed Pepper Stew 144

Spicy Prawn and Tomato Curry 146

Hot, Sweet and Sour Salmon 160

Creamy Beetroot, Green Bean and Tomato Curry 184

Mango and Coconut Curry 186

Sweet Potato and Lychee Curry 190

Carrot, Pea and Potato Curry 204

Butternut Squash and Red Pepper Curry 212

Spiced Okra, Tomato and Coconut 218

Spicy Chickpea Curry 274

Mild to Medium

A subtle hint of spice to tempt every palate

Thai Green Chicken Curry 46

Curried Chicken and Peas 62

Pork, Red Pepper and Pea Curry 90

West Indian Curried Beef and Black Bean Stew 120

Creamy Curried Mussel Soup 132

Prawn, Lemon Grass and Mango Curry 164

Yellow Fish, Potato and Tomato Curry 172

Spinach, Tomato and Paneer Curry 202

Curried Mushrooms and Tomatoes 208

Middle Eastern Courgette, Tomato and Mint Curry 214

Thai Massaman Pumpkin Curry 226

Carrot and Black Bean Curry 242

Food for Friends

Wholesome, hearty meals perfect for a get-together

Cold Roast Chicken with Spicy Salsa Verde 28

Sweet and Spicy Chicken Noodles 52

Spicy Chicken, Mushroom and Spinach Pancakes 58

Chicken, Chilli and Rosemary Soup 60

Curried Chicken and Grape Salad 66

Chinese Turkey Chow Mein 70

Chinese Beef with Tofu and Vegetables 78

Grilled Tandoori Lamb Chops 84

Hot and Spicy Steak and Rocket Ciabattas 86

Spicy Lamb and Herb Kebabs 100

Spicy Eggs with Merguez Sausages and Tomato 102

Five-Spice Pork Chops with Green Beans 122

QuickCook
Poultry

Recipes listed by cooking time

30

20

10

30 Green Chicken Skewers with Cucumber and Chilli Dip

Serves 4

800 g (1¾ lb) boneless, skinless chicken thighs, cut into bite-sized pieces
30 g (1 oz) chopped coriander
30 g (1 oz) chopped mint leaves
1 teaspoon coarse black pepper
juice of 2 lemons
1 teaspoon light muscovado sugar
2 teaspoons peeled and finely grated fresh root ginger
2 garlic cloves, crushed
200 ml (7 fl oz) natural yogurt
lemon wedges, to serve

For the dip

125 ml (4 fl oz) rice or wine vinegar
2 tablespoons caster sugar
1 red chilli, finely diced
½ red onion, finely diced
6 tablespoons finely diced cucumber

- Put the chicken in a shallow non-reactive bowl. Put the herbs, pepper, lemon juice, sugar, ginger, garlic and yogurt in a food processor or blender and blend until smooth. Pour the mixture over the chicken and toss to coat evenly, then cover and leave to marinate for 10–15 minutes.

- Meanwhile, make the dip. Heat the vinegar and sugar in a small saucepan until the sugar has dissolved, then increase the heat and boil for 3 minutes until slightly syrupy. Remove from the heat and stir in the red chilli and red onion. Leave to cool. When cool, stir in the cucumber and set aside.

- Thread the chicken on to 12 metal skewers, then cook under a preheated medium-hot grill for 4–5 minutes on each side or until cooked through.

- Transfer the skewers on to 4 serving plates and drizzle over a little of the dip. Serve with the remaining dip and lemon wedges to squeeze over.

 Warm Green Chicken and Rice Salad

Heat a large nonstick wok, add a 600 g (1 lb 5 oz) tub ready-cooked pilau rice and stir-fry over a high heat for 3–4 minutes until piping hot. Remove from the heat. Stir in 400 g (13 oz) ready-cooked chicken breasts, skin removed and diced, 1 deseeded, finely chopped red chilli and a large handful each of chopped mint and coriander. Transfer to a large bowl, squeeze over the juice of 1 lime, season and toss to mix well.

 Green Chicken Stir-Fry

Heat 2 tablespoons sunflower oil in a large wok or frying pan until hot, add 8 sliced spring onions, 2 chopped garlic cloves and 2 teaspoons peeled and grated fresh root ginger and stir-fry over a medium-high heat for 2–3 minutes. Add 600 g (1 lb 5 oz) boneless, skinless chicken breasts, thinly sliced, and stir-fry for a further 5–6 minutes or until just cooked through. Add a 300 g (10 oz) pack ready-cooked rice noodles and stir-fry for another 2–3 minutes or until piping hot. Remove from the heat and stir in a large handful each of finely chopped mint and coriander. Serve immediately.

30 Chicken, Lemon and Tarragon Risotto

Serves 4

50 g (2 oz) unsalted butter
1 tablespoon olive oil
1 onion, finely chopped
1 red chilli, deseeded and
  finely chopped
2 garlic cloves, finely chopped
1 celery stick, finely chopped
1 carrot, peeled and finely chopped
275 g (9 oz) risotto rice
100 ml (3½ fl oz) dry white wine
3 shop-bought ready-cooked
  chicken breasts, skin removed
  and diced
900 ml (1½ pints) hot
  vegetable stock
100 g (3½ oz) finely grated
  Parmesan cheese
finely grated rind of 1 lemon
6 tablespoons finely
  chopped tarragon
salt and pepper

• Heat the butter and oil in a large frying pan, add the onion, chilli, garlic, celery and carrot and cook over a medium heat for 3–4 minutes until softened. Add the rice and stir for 1 minute or until the grains are well coated. Pour in the wine and stir until it has been absorbed, then stir in the chicken.

• Add 1 ladle of hot stock and simmer, stirring until it has been absorbed. Repeat with another ladle of stock, then continue to add the stock at intervals and cook as before, for a further 18–20 minutes or until the liquid has been absorbed and the rice is tender but still firm (al dente). Reserve 1 ladle of stock.

• Add the reserved stock, Parmesan, lemon rind and tarragon, season and mix well. Remove from the heat, cover and leave to stand for 2 minutes.

• Spoon into warm bowls, season and serve immediately.

 Chicken, Lemon and Tarragon Baguettes

Slice 2 warm medium baguettes into half horizontally and spread each with 2 tablespoons shop-bought tarragon mayonnaise. Divide 2 shop-bought ready-cooked chicken breasts, skin removed and sliced, between the baguette bases, then sprinkle over the finely grated rind of ½ lemon and season. Top with the baguette lids, then cut each into 2 and serve.

 Grilled Chicken with Chilli, Lemon and Tarragon Butter

Mix together 150 g (5 oz) softened butter, 1 deseeded and finely diced red chilli, the finely grated rind and juice of 1 lemon, 1 crushed garlic clove and 4 tablespoons very finely chopped tarragon in a bowl. Meanwhile, season 4 large boneless, skin-on chicken breasts and cook under a preheated hot grill for

6–8 minutes on each side or until cooked through. Serve with the flavoured butter and a crisp green salad.

 # Cold Roast Chicken with Spicy Salsa Verde

Serves 4

1 x 1.5 kg (3 lb) shop-bought
  ready-cooked roast chicken

For the spicy salsa verde

2 tablespoons red wine vinegar
40 g (1½ oz) flat leaf parsley
  leaves, chopped
20 g (¾ oz) basil or mint leaves,
  chopped
2 garlic cloves, crushed
2 red chillies, deseeded and
  finely chopped
4 anchovy fillets in oil, drained
  and chopped
2 tablespoons salted capers, rinsed
125 ml (4 fl oz) extra-virgin olive
  oil, plus extra if needed
pepper

- To make the spicy salsa verde, pour the vinegar into the bowl of a mini food processor, then add the herbs and pulse to form a coarse paste. Add the garlic, red chillies, anchovies and capers and whizz again to a coarse paste. Gradually add the oil with the motor running, but do not over-process. Season with pepper.

- To serve, joint the chicken and transfer on to 4 plates. Spoon over the spicy salsa verde and serve.

 Pan-Fried Chicken with Spicy Salsa Verde Make the salsa verde as above and set aside. Lay 4 large boneless chicken breasts, skin-on, between 2 sheets of clingfilm and flatten with a rolling pin or meat mallet until 1 cm (½ inch) thick. Season and drizzle with 2 tablespoons olive oil. Heat a large nonstick frying pan until hot, add the chicken breasts, skin-side down, and fry for 4–5 minutes on each side or until cooked through. Serve with the salsa verde.

 Poached Chicken with Spicy Salsa Verde Put large 4 boneless, skinless chicken breasts in a large saucepan and pour over 800 ml (1 pint 8 fl oz) hot chicken stock. Add 1 bay leaf, 1 chopped carrot, 2 chopped celery sticks and 1 quartered onion. Bring to the boil, then reduce the heat to medium and cook, uncovered, for 20 minutes or until the chicken is cooked through. Meanwhile, make the salsa verde as above. Remove the chicken from the pan with a slotted spoon and drain on kitchen paper. Slice the chicken and serve with the salsa verde.

30 Griddled Chicken with Chilli and Rocket Pesto

Serves 4

600 g (1 lb 5 oz) midi vine
tomatoes
4 large boneless, skinless
chicken breasts
olive oil, for brushing
salt and pepper

For the pesto

4 garlic cloves, crushed
2 red chillies, deseeded and
finely chopped
30 g (1 oz) basil leaves
40 g (1 oz) rocket leaves
50 g (2 oz) Parmesan
cheese, grated
100 g (3½ oz) pine nuts, toasted
150 ml (¼ pint) extra-virgin olive
oil, plus extra if needed

- Brush the tomatoes with oil and season well. Place on a nonstick baking sheet and cook in a preheated oven, 220°C (425°F), Gas Mark 7, for 10–12 minutes.

- Meanwhile, lay a chicken breast between 2 sheets of clingfilm and flatten slightly with a rolling pin or meat mallet. Repeat with the remaining chicken breasts. Brush lightly with oil and season. Heat a griddle pan until smoking hot, add the chicken and cook for 5–6 minutes on each side or until cooked through. Remove the chicken and leave to rest for 2–3 minutes.

- While the chicken is cooking, make the pesto. Put all the ingredients in a food processor or blender and blend until fairly smooth, adding a little more oil for a runnier consistency if liked.

- Transfer the chicken on to warm serving plates, drizzle over the pesto and serve with the roasted vine tomatoes.

 Chicken Salad with Chilli and Rocket Pesto Make the pesto as above. Put 4 shop-bought ready-cooked chicken breasts, skin removed and thinly sliced, and 400 g (13 oz) halved midi vine tomatoes in a salad bowl. Drizzle over the pesto, toss to mix well and serve.

 Chicken with Chilli and Rocket Pesto Linguine Cook 375 g (12 oz) dried linguine in a large saucepan of salted boiling water according to the packet instructions until al dente. Meanwhile, make the pesto as above and cut 2 large shop-bought skinless ready-cooked chicken breasts into 1 cm (½ inch) pieces. Put the chicken and 200 g (7 oz) quartered midi vine tomatoes in a large bowl. Drain the pasta, then add to the chicken mixture. Add the pesto, toss to mix well and serve immediately.

30 Harissa-Spiced Turkey and Mixed Pepper Skewers

Serves 4

400 g (13 oz) turkey breast fillets, cut into bite-sized pieces
4 tablespoons harissa paste
1 tablespoon finely grated garlic
1 tablespoon peeled and finely grated fresh root ginger
juice of 2 lemons
1 red pepper, cored, deseeded and cut into bite-sized pieces
1 yellow pepper, cored, deseeded and cut into bite-sized pieces
250 g (8 oz) couscous
4 tablespoons finely chopped parsley, plus extra to garnish
salt and pepper

- Put the turkey in a large non-reactive bowl. Mix together the harissa, garlic, ginger and lemon juice in a small bowl, then season well. Pour the mixture over the turkey, toss to coat evenly, then cover and leave to marinate for 10 minutes.

- Thread the turkey on to 8 metal skewers, alternating with the red and yellow peppers. Cook under a preheated medium-hot grill for 6–8 minutes on each side or until the edges are lightly charred in places and the turkey is cooked through.

- Meanwhile, put the couscous in a large heatproof bowl and season with salt. Pour over boiling water to just cover, then cover with clingfilm and leave to stand for 8–10 minutes, or according to the packet instructions, until the water is absorbed. Gently fork to separate the grains, then set aside and keep warm.

- Spoon the couscous on to 4 serving plates and sprinkle with the parsley. Top each with 2 skewers and serve scattered with extra parsley.

---

10 Turkey Ciabattas with Harissa Mayo

Halve and toast 4 ciabatta rolls. Meanwhile, mix together 1 tablespoon harissa paste, 8 tablespoons mayonnaise and the juice of ½ lemon in a bowl, then spread over the toasted ciabatta bases. Divide ¼ cucumber, thinly sliced, 4 plum tomatoes, thinly sliced, and 400 g (13 oz) shop-bought ready-cooked sliced turkey breast between the bases and top with the ciabatta lids. Serve with fries.

20 Turkey, Mixed Pepper and Harissa Stir-Fry

Core, deseed and thinly slice 1 red pepper and 1 yellow pepper. Heat 2 tablespoons sunflower oil in a large wok or frying pan until hot, add the peppers and 400 g (13 oz) turkey breast fillets, thinly sliced, and stir-fry over a high heat for 6–8 minutes or until the turkey is just cooked through. Add 1 thinly sliced red onion and 8 finely sliced spring onions and stir-fry for a further 3–4 minutes. Mix together 2 tablespoons harissa paste and 4 tablespoons passata, then add to the wok or pan and cook for 1–2 minutes or until piping hot. Serve with herbed couscous or rice.

10 Spicy Chicken and Mango Noodles

Serves 4

2 tablespoons vegetable oil

2 tablespoons hot chilli sauce

4 tablespoons sweet chilli sauce

4 tablespoons dark soy sauce

2 large boneless, skinless chicken breasts, cut into thin strips

200 g (7 oz) pack fresh mango chunks

300 g (10 oz) pack ready-prepared stir-fry vegetables

2 x 300 g (10 oz) packs ready-cooked medium egg noodles

75 g (3 oz) dry-roasted peanuts, chopped

salt and pepper

- Mix together the oil, hot chilli sauce, sweet chilli sauce and soy sauce in a large bowl. Add the chicken strips, season and mix together.

- Heat a large nonstick wok or frying pan until hot, then add the chicken, reserving the marinade, and stir-fry over a high heat for 5 minutes or until lightly browned and cooked through. Add the mango, stir-fry vegetables, noodles and the reserved marinade and stir-fry for a further few minutes until piping hot.

- Mix in the chopped peanuts, then divide between 4 warm bowls. Serve immediately.

---

20 Spicy Chicken and Mango Skewers

Cut 4 large boneless, skinless chicken breasts into bite-sized pieces and place in a bowl with 1 tablespoon hot chilli sauce, 2 tablespoons sweet chilli sauce and 2 tablespoons light soy sauce. Stir to mix well. Thread the chicken on to 12 metal skewers, alternating with 400 g (13 oz) shop-bought fresh mango chunks. Cook under a preheated medium-hot grill for 4–5 minutes on each side or until the chicken is cooked through. Serve with a mixed leaf salad.

30 Chicken and Mango Curry

Heat 2 tablespoons sunflower oil in a large wok or frying pan until hot, add 1 chopped onion and stir-fry over a medium heat for 4–5 minutes until softened. Add 2 chopped garlic cloves, 1 teaspoon peeled and grated fresh root ginger, 1 deseeded and chopped red chilli and 1 tablespoon medium or hot curry powder and stir-fry for a further 1–2 minutes, then add 600 g (1 lb 5 oz) boneless, skinless chicken breasts, cubed, and stir-fry for 1–2 minutes or until lightly browned. Pour in a 400 ml (14 fl oz) can coconut milk and bring to the boil, then reduce the heat to medium and cook, stirring frequently, for 10–12 minutes. Add 400 g (13 oz) shop-bought fresh mango chunks and cook for a further 3–4 minutes or until the chicken is cooked through. Scatter over 4 tablespoons chopped coriander leaves and serve immediately with steamed rice.

Piquant Chicken and Mixed Pepper Brochettes

Serves 4

800 g (1¾ lb) boneless, skinless
   chicken breasts, cut into
   bite-sized pieces
finely grated rind and juice
   of 1 lemon
1 red chilli, deseeded and
   finely chopped
1 teaspoon hot smoked paprika
100 ml (3½ fl oz) extra-virgin
   olive oil
1 tablespoon dried oregano
3 garlic cloves, crushed
1 onion, cut into large pieces
1 red pepper, cored, deseeded and
   cut into large pieces
1 yellow pepper, cored, deseeded
   and cut into large pieces
salt and pepper
lemon wedges, to serve (optional)

- Put the chicken in a shallow non-reactive bowl. Mix together the lemon rind and juice, chilli, smoked paprika, oil, oregano and garlic in a bowl, then season well. Pour the mixture over the chicken and toss to coat evenly.

- Thread the chicken on to 8 metal skewers, alternating with the onion and red or yellow peppers. Cook under a preheated medium-hot grill for 4–5 minutes on each side or until the chicken is cooked through.

- Transfer the brochettes to 4 serving plates and serve with lemon wedges to squeeze over, if liked.

Piquant Chicken and Mixed Pepper Salad

Put 4 shop-bought ready-cooked chicken breasts, skin removed and roughly shredded, 400 g (13 oz) drained mixed roasted peppers from a jar and a handful of wild rocket leaves in a large salad bowl. Mix together 1 teaspoon chilli paste, 6 tablespoons extra-virgin olive oil, 1 teaspoon runny honey and the juice of 1 large lemon in a bowl, then season. Pour the dressing over the salad, toss to mix well and serve.

Piquant Chicken and Mixed Pepper Pot

Heat 2 tablespoons sunflower oil in a large heavy-based saucepan, add 1 chopped red onion and cook over a medium heat for 2–3 minutes, stirring occasionally, until beginning to soften. Add 4 chopped garlic cloves and 1 deseeded and chopped red chilli and fry, stirring, for a further 1–2 minutes. Stir in 4 large boneless, skinless chicken breasts, thickly sliced, 1 cored, deseeded and thickly sliced red pepper and 1 cored, deseeded and thickly sliced yellow pepper and cook, stirring, until the chicken is lightly browned, then pour in 500 ml (17 fl oz) hot chicken stock and bring to the boil. Reduce the heat to medium and cook, uncovered, for 15–20 minutes or until the chicken is cooked through and the peppers are tender. Season, then serve with warm crusty bread.

3① Spanish Turkey Stew with Lemon and Chilli

Serves 4

800 g (1¾ lb) turkey breast steaks, cut into bite-sized pieces
2 tablespoons sunflower oil
4 garlic cloves, crushed
1 onion, finely chopped
2 teaspoons dried red chilli flakes
10–12 baby onions, peeled
2 carrots, peeled and cut into bite-sized pieces
2 potatoes, peeled and cut into bite-sized pieces
1 tablespoon sweet smoked paprika
3 tablespoons lemon juice
6 tablespoons finely chopped flat leaf parsley
500 ml (17 fl oz) hot chicken stock
salt and pepper
crusty bread, to serve

- Put the turkey in a bowl and season well. Heat the oil in a large frying pan, add the turkey and cook over a high heat, stirring occasionally, for 2–3 minutes or until browned all over.

- Transfer to a heavy-based saucepan, stir in the remaining ingredients and bring to the boil. Reduce the heat to medium and cook, uncovered, for 20 minutes or until the turkey is cooked through and the vegetables are tender.

- Ladle into warm bowls and serve with crusty bread.

1① Quick Turkey, Chilli and Lemon Rice

Heat 2 tablespoons sunflower oil in a large frying pan until hot, add 4 chopped garlic cloves, 1 deseeded and chopped red chilli and ½ small chopped onion. Stir-fry for 1–2 minutes. Add 500 g (1 lb) shop-bought ready-cooked rice, 1 tablespoon smoked paprika and 400 g (13 oz) shop-bought ready-cooked diced turkey breast and stir-fry for a further 3–4 minutes until piping hot. Remove from the heat, season and stir in the grated rind of ½ lemon and 4 tablespoons chopped flat leaf parsley.

2① Turkey, Chilli and Lemon Stir-Fry

Heat 2 tablespoons sunflower oil in a large wok or frying pan until hot, add 2 finely sliced onions, 2 deseeded and finely sliced red chillies, 1 teaspoon peeled and grated fresh root ginger and 3 chopped garlic cloves and stir-fry over a high heat for 4–5 minutes. Add 600 g (1 lb 5 oz) turkey breast fillets, thinly sliced, and stir-fry for a further 6–8 minutes or until cooked through. Stir in 4 tablespoons light soy sauce, 2 tablespoons sweet chilli sauce and the finely grated rind and juice of 1 lemon. Season, then serve immediately with steamed rice or noodles.

20 Spicy Chicken, Apricot and Cranberry Couscous

Serves 4

200 g (7 oz) couscous
1 tablespoon hot curry powder
5 tablespoons extra-virgin olive oil
700 ml (1 pint 3 fl oz) hot
    chicken stock
100 g (3½ oz) cashew nuts
finely grated rind and juice of
    1 lemon
1 red chilli, deseeded and chopped
4 tablespoons chopped mint leaves
4 tablespoons chopped coriander
100 g (3½ oz) ready-to-eat dried
    apricots, finely chopped
100 g (3½ oz) dried cranberries
2 shop-bought ready-cooked
    chicken breasts, skin removed
    and roughly shredded
juice of 1 orange
salt and pepper
flat leaf parsley, chopped, to serve

- Put the couscous, curry powder and oil in a large heatproof bowl. Stir in the stock, then cover with clingfilm and leave to stand for 8–10 minutes, or according to the packet instructions, until the stock is absorbed.

- Meanwhile, heat a small nonstick frying pan until hot, add the cashew nuts and dry-fry, stirring frequently, for 3–4 minutes or until toasted. Remove from the pan and set aside.

- Gently fork the couscous to separate the grains, then stir in the cashews and all the remaining ingredients. Season, toss to mix well and serve scattered with chopped parsley.

 Spicy Chicken and Fruit Couscous Salad

Put 400 g (13 oz) shop-bought ready-cooked chicken breasts, skin removed and shredded, and 2 x 250 g (8 oz) tubs ready-cooked roasted vegetable couscous in a large bowl. Mix together 4 tablespoons olive oil, 1 deseeded and finely diced red chilli, 50 g (2 oz) chopped dried apricots, 50 g (2 oz) dried cranberries, 1 teaspoon hot curry powder and the juice of 2 limes in a bowl and season. Pour over the salad, toss and serve.

 Fruity Chicken Tagine

Put 350 g (11½ oz) couscous in a large heatproof bowl. Add boiling water to just cover, then cover with clingfilm and leave to stand for 8–10 minutes, or according to the packet instructions, until all the water is absorbed. Meanwhile, heat 2 tablespoons olive oil in a large frying pan, add 1 tablespoon hot curry powder, 1 chopped onion, 2 chopped garlic cloves and 1 tablespoon peeled and finely grated fresh root ginger and cook over a high heat, stirring, for 1 minute. Add 700 g (1½ lb) boneless, skinless chicken thighs, diced, and fry for a further 1–2 minutes until browned, then pour over 600 ml (1 pint) hot chicken stock and bring to the boil. Stir in 300 g (10 oz) dried apricots and 200 g (7 oz) sultanas, reduce the heat to medium and cook, covered, for 20 minutes until cooked through. Stir in 1 tablespoon harissa paste and a handful of chopped coriander and season. Serve with the couscous.

30 Spiced Chicken Stew with Preserved Lemon

Serves 4

2 tablespoons olive oil

800 g (1¾ lb) boneless, skinless chicken breasts, cut into bite-sized pieces

1 large onion, thinly sliced

4 garlic cloves, finely chopped

1 teaspoon peeled and finely grated fresh root ginger

1 red chilli, deseeded and finely chopped

2 teaspoons ground cumin

3 cinnamon sticks

¼ teaspoon ground turmeric

2 large carrots, peeled and cut into bite-sized pieces

large pinch of saffron threads

750 ml (1¼ pints) hot chicken stock

1 tablespoon rose harissa paste

8 green olives, pitted

8 black olives, pitted

6 small preserved lemons, halved

salt and pepper

- Heat the oil in a large heavy-based saucepan, add the chicken and onion and cook over a high heat, stirring occasionally, for 2–3 minutes until browned. Add the garlic, ginger, red chilli, cumin, cinnamon sticks and turmeric and fry, stirring, for 30 seconds.

- Add the carrots, saffron and stock and bring to the boil. Reduce the heat to medium and cook, uncovered, for 15–20 minutes or until the chicken is cooked through and the carrots are tender.

- Add the harissa, olives and preserved lemons, season to taste and stir to mix well. Ladle into warm bowls and serve immediately.

---

10 Spicy Lemon Chicken Salad

Put 4 shop-bought ready-cooked chicken breasts, skin removed and roughly shredded, and the leaves from 1 Romaine lettuce in a large serving dish. Mix together the juice of 1 lemon, 2 tablespoons finely chopped preserved lemons, 2 teaspoons harissa paste, 1 tablespoon runny honey and 6 tablespoons olive oil in a bowl. Season and serve with the salad.

20 Spicy Chicken and Preserved Lemon

Skewers Mix together 1 tablespoon harissa paste, 2 tablespoons finely chopped preserved lemons, the juice of 2 lemons and 1 tablespoon runny honey in a large non-reactive bowl. Add 800 g (1¾ lb) boneless, skinless chicken breasts, cubed, and toss to coat evenly. Season, then cover and leave to marinate for a few minutes. When ready to cook, thread the chicken on to 8 metal skewers and cook under a medium-hot grill for 6–8 minutes on each side or until cooked through. Serve with couscous or steamed rice.

20 Spicy Vietnamese Chicken

Serves 4

3 tablespoons sunflower oil

800 g (1¾ lb) boneless, skinless
 chicken breasts, cut into strips

12 spring onions, cut into 3 cm
 (1 inch) lengths

4 garlic cloves, finely chopped

1 red chilli, deseeded and
 finely sliced

2 star anise

8 cm (3 inch) length of trimmed
 lemon grass stalk, finely chopped

1 teaspoon crushed cardamom
 seeds

1 cinnamon stick

300 g (10 oz) mangetout, sliced

1 carrot, peeled and cut into batons

2 tablespoons fish sauce

3 tablespoons oyster sauce

To garnish

handful of chopped
 coriander leaves

handful of chopped mint leaves

chopped roasted peanuts

- Heat half the oil in a large wok or frying pan until hot, add the chicken and stir-fry over a high heat for 3–4 minutes or until lightly browned and just cooked through. Remove with a slotted spoon and keep warm.

- Heat the remaining oil in the wok or pan until hot, add the spring onions and stir-fry for 1–2 minutes until softened. Add the garlic, red chilli, star anise, lemon grass, cardamom, cinnamon stick, mangetout and carrot and stir-fry for a further 3–4 minutes or until the vegetables are softened.

- Return the chicken to the wok or pan with the fish sauce and oyster sauce and continue to stir-fry for 3–4 minutes or until the chicken is cooked through and piping hot.

- Spoon into warm bowls, scatter with chopped herbs and peanuts and serve immediately.

---

10 Vietnamese Chicken Soup

Put 800 ml (1 pint 8 fl oz) shop-bought fresh chicken stock, 1 tablespoon lemon grass paste, 1 teaspoon chilli paste, 1 teaspoon garlic paste and 1 teaspoon ground cinnamon in a pan and bring to the boil. Stir in 400 g (13 oz) shop-bought ready-cooked chicken breasts, shredded, and cook for 1–2 minutes or until piping hot.

30 Vietnamese Grilled Chicken

Chop 800 g (1¾ lb) boneless, skinless chicken thighs into large pieces and put in a large bowl. Mix together the juice of 2 limes, a 2 cm (¾ inch) length of trimmed lemon grass stalk, chopped, 2 tablespoons fish sauce, 1 tablespoon garlic paste, 2 deseeded and diced red chillies, 2 tablespoons caster sugar and 2 tablespoons sunflower oil in a bowl. Pour the mixture over the chicken, toss to coat evenly, then cover and leave to marinate for 5 minutes. Put the chicken on an oiled grill rack in a single layer, brushing over any remaining marinade, and cook under a preheated medium-hot grill for 6–8 minutes on each side or until cooked through. Serve with steamed rice.

30 Thai Green Chicken Curry

Serves 4

400 ml (14 fl oz) can coconut milk
100 g (3½ oz) chopped coriander
1 tablespoon sunflower oil
3 tablespoons Thai green
    curry paste
2 green chillies, deseeded and
    finely chopped
800 g (1¾ lb) boneless, skinless
    chicken thighs, cut into
    bite-sized pieces
200 ml (7 fl oz) hot chicken stock
6 kaffir lime leaves
2 tablespoons fish sauce
1 tablespoon grated palm sugar or
    caster sugar
200 g (7 oz) Thai baby
    aubergines, halved if large, or
    cut into 1.5 cm (¾ inch) cubes
100 g (3½ oz) green beans, trimmed
juice of 1 lime
red chilli slivers, to garnish
steamed jasmine rice, to serve

- Put the coconut milk and coriander in a food processor or blender and blend until well mixed. Strain the mixture into a jug using a fine sieve and discard the coriander.

- Heat the oil in a large wok or heavy-based saucepan until hot, add the curry paste and green chillies and stir-fry over a high heat for 2–3 minutes. Add the chicken and stir-fry for a further 5–6 minutes or until lightly browned.

- Stir in the coconut milk mixture, stock, lime leaves, fish sauce, sugar and aubergine, then reduce the heat and simmer, uncovered, for 10–15 minutes, stirring occasionally, until the chicken is cooked through. Add the green beans and simmer for a further 2–3 minutes or until tender.

- Remove from the heat and stir in the lime juice. Ladle into warm bowls, sprinkle with red chilli slivers and serve with steamed jasmine rice.

Thai Green Chicken Stir-Fry

Heat 2 tablespoons sunflower oil in a large wok until hot, add 2 tablespoons Thai green curry paste and stir-fry over a medium heat for 1 minute. Increase the heat to high, add 600 g (1 lb 5 oz) boneless, skinless chicken breasts, sliced, and 200 ml (7 fl oz) canned coconut milk and stir-fry for 5–6 minutes until the chicken is just cooked through. Serve with steamed rice.

Grilled Thai Green Chicken

Mix together 1 tablespoon Thai green curry paste, 100 ml (3½ fl oz) coconut cream and the juice of 1 lime in a bowl. Make 3–4 slashes on 4 large boneless, skinless chicken breasts, then spread the mixture all over the chicken and into the slashes and season with salt. Cook under a preheated medium-hot grill for 6–8 minutes on each side or until the chicken is cooked through. Serve with steamed rice, salad or noodles.

HOT-POUL-GOG

30 Thai Red Duck Curry

Serves 4

2 tablespoons sunflower oil

2 garlic cloves, crushed

1 teaspoon peeled and finely
   grated fresh root ginger

2 tablespoons Thai red curry
   paste

400 g (13 oz) skinless duck
   breasts, thinly sliced

400 ml (14 fl oz) can coconut milk

200 g (7 oz) mangetout, halved
   lengthways

200 ml (7 fl oz) hot chicken stock

4 kaffir lime leaves

2 teaspoons grated palm sugar or
   caster sugar

2 lemon grass stalks, bruised

salt and pepper

chopped coriander leaves,
   to garnish

steamed jasmine rice, to serve

- Heat the oil in a large wok or frying pan until hot, add the garlic and ginger and stir-fry over a high heat for 20–30 seconds. Stir in the curry paste and stir-fry for 30 seconds, then add the duck and stir-fry for a further 4–5 minutes.

- Stir in the coconut milk, mangetout, stock, lime leaves, sugar and lemon grass and bring to the boil, then reduce the heat to medium and cook, uncovered, for 15–20 minutes, stirring occasionally, until the duck is cooked through. Season to taste.

- Ladle into warm bowls, scatter with chopped coriander and serve with steamed jasmine rice.

 **Thai-Style Red
Duck Salad**

Thinly slice 4 smoked duck breasts and put in a large salad bowl with a large handful of mixed salad leaves. Mix together 1 teaspoon Thai red curry paste, 6 tablespoons light olive oil, 2 teaspoons runny honey and 3 tablespoons red wine vinegar in a bowl, then season. Pour the dressing over the salad, toss to mix well and serve with warm crusty bread.

 **Grilled Thai
Red Duck**

Mix together 1 tablespoon Thai red curry paste and 100 ml (3½ fl oz) coconut cream in a bowl. Using a sharp knife, score the skin side of 4 large duck breasts, then spread the red curry mixture all over the breasts and season. Place the duck in a single layer, skin-side up, on an oiled grill rack and cook under a preheated medium grill for 4–5 minutes on each side or

until cooked to your liking. Serve with steamed rice and Chinese greens.

30 Thai Green Coconut-Stuffed Chicken

Serves 4

4 large boneless chicken breasts,
  skin-on
1 teaspoon Thai green curry paste
4 tablespoons coconut cream
2 tablespoons fresh white
  breadcrumbs
finely grated rind of 1 lime
1 teaspoon lemon grass paste
sunflower oil, for drizzling
salt and pepper

To serve

steamed jasmine rice
steamed Chinese greens

- Using a small, sharp knife, cut a slit down the side of each chicken breast to form a deep pocket. Mix together the remaining ingredients in a bowl, then season well. Divide the mixture evenly between the 4 chicken pockets.

- Drizzle with a little oil, then transfer to a nonstick baking sheet. Place in a preheated oven, 180°C (350°F), Gas Mark 4, for 18–20 minutes or until the chicken is cooked through.

- Serve with steamed jasmine rice and Chinese greens.

Quick Thai Green Chicken Curry

Heat 2 tablespoons sunflower oil in a large wok or frying pan until hot, add 2 tablespoons Thai green curry paste and stir-fry over a medium heat for 1–2 minutes. Stir in 4 shop-bought ready-cooked chicken breasts, skin removed and diced, and a 400 ml (14 fl oz) can coconut milk and bring to the boil. Cook for 3–4 minutes or until piping hot, then remove from the heat, season and stir in 4 tablespoons each of chopped coriander and thai basil leaves. Serve with steamed rice or noodles.

Thai Green Chicken Fried Rice

Heat 2 tablespoons sunflower oil in a large wok or frying pan until hot, add 6 sliced spring onions, 1 chopped garlic clove, 1 teaspoon peeled and grated fresh root ginger, a 2 cm (¾ inch) length of trimmed lemon grass stalk, finely chopped, and 1 tablespoon Thai green curry paste and stir-fry over a high heat for 1–2 minutes. Stir in 100 ml (3½ fl oz) coconut cream, 500 g (1 lb) shop-bought ready-cooked basmati rice and 4 shop-bought ready-cooked chicken breasts, skin removed and thinly sliced, then reduce the heat to medium and stir-fry for 7–8 minutes or until piping hot. Season, then serve immediately.

 Sweet and Spicy Chicken Noodles

Serves 4

300 g (10 oz) dried medium
   egg noodles
2 tablespoons sunflower oil
400 g (13 oz) boneless, skinless
   chicken breasts, cut into cubes
300 g (10 oz) pack ready-
   prepared stir-fry vegetables
2 red chillies, deseeded and sliced
1 garlic clove, crushed
1 tablespoon cornflour
6 tablespoons light soy sauce
5 tablespoons sweet chilli sauce
1 tablespoon rice wine vinegar
4 tablespoons passata
1 tablespoon soft light brown sugar
½ teaspoon ground ginger
50 ml (2 fl oz) water
200 g (7 oz) pineapple flesh, cut
   into small pieces
4 spring onions, thinly sliced

- Cook the noodles according to the packet instructions, then drain and keep warm.

- Meanwhile, heat the oil in a large wok or frying pan until hot, add the chicken and stir-fry over a medium-high heat for 6–8 minutes or until lightly browned and just cooked through. Add the stir-fry vegetables and stir-fry for a further 3–4 minutes.

- Mix together the red chillies, garlic, cornflour, soy sauce, chilli sauce, vinegar, passata, sugar and ground ginger in a small bowl. Add this mixture to the wok with the measurement water, pineapple and spring onions and stir-fry for 2–3 minutes or until all the ingredients are well coated.

- Add the reserved noodles to the wok, toss to mix well and heat until piping hot. Divide into warm bowls and serve immediately.

 Sweet and Spicy Chicken and Pea Rice

Heat 2 tablespoons sunflower oil in a large wok until hot, add 500 g (1 lb) shop-bought ready-cooked rice, 300 g (10 oz) frozen peas, 1 tablespoon sweet chilli sauce, 4 tablespoons light soy sauce, 1 tablespoon garlic paste and 1 tablespoon ginger paste and stir-fry over a high heat for 4–5 minutes. Add 400 g (13 oz) shop-bought ready-cooked chicken breasts, diced, and stir-fry for 2–3 minutes or until piping hot.

 Sweet and Spicy Chicken Drumsticks

Make 3–4 deep slashes in 12 large chicken drumsticks and put in an ovenproof casserole dish. Mix together 3 deseeded and sliced red chillies, 2 crushed garlic cloves, 8 tablespoons light soy sauce, 5 tablespoons sweet chilli sauce, 2 tablespoons rice wine vinegar, 1 tablespoon soft light brown sugar, 4 tablespoons sunflower oil and 1 teaspoon ground ginger in a bowl. Pour the mixture over the chicken and toss to coat evenly. Place in a preheated oven, 220°C (425°F), Gas Mark 7, for 20–25 minutes or until the chicken is cooked through. Serve with noodles or steamed rice.

30 Rose Harissa and Chicken Meatball Tagine

Serves 4

2 teaspoons finely peeled and
grated fresh root ginger
4 teaspoons finely grated garlic
1 teaspoon ground cinnamon
35 g (1½ oz) finely chopped
coriander leaves, plus extra
to garnish
800g (1¾ lb) minced chicken
3 tablespoons sunflower oil
1 onion, finely chopped
2 tablespoons rose harissa paste
400 g (14 oz) can chopped
tomatoes
200 ml (7 fl oz) hot chicken stock
salt and pepper
couscous, to serve

- Put the ginger, garlic, cinnamon, coriander and chicken in a mixing bowl, then season well. Using your hands, mix well to combine, then roll and shape tablespoons of the mixture into bite-sized balls.

- Heat 2 tablespoons of the oil in a large frying pan until hot, add the chicken balls and cook in batches until lightly browned. Remove with a slotted spoon and set aside.

- Add the remaining oil to the pan, add the onion and cook, stirring, over a medium heat for 1–2 minutes, then stir in the harissa paste and cook for a further 1–2 minutes. Stir in the tomatoes and stock and bring to the boil, then reduce the heat to medium and cook, uncovered, for 10 minutes.

- Return the chicken balls to the pan and stir gently to coat with the sauce. Simmer gently for 5–6 minutes or until piping hot and cooked through.

- Spoon into warm bowls, scatter with chopped coriander and serve with couscous.

 Quick Rose Harissa and Chicken Sauté

Heat 1 tablespoon sunflower oil in a large frying pan, add 600 g (1 lb 5 oz) minced chicken and fry over a high heat for 4–5 minutes or until sealed and browned. Stir in 3 tablespoons rose harissa paste and 200 g (7 oz) frozen peas and fry for a further 2–3 minutes or until cooked through and piping hot, then remove from the heat. Stir in 4 tablespoons chopped coriander leaves and serve with rice or crusty bread.

 Grilled Rose Harissa Chicken

Mix together 2 tablespoons rose harissa paste, the juice of 1 lemon and 4 tablespoons natural yogurt in a small bowl, then season with salt. Make 3–4 deep slashes in 4 boneless, skinless chicken breasts using a small, sharp knife and spread the mixture all over the chicken and into the cuts. Transfer the chicken to a lightly oiled grill rack and cook under a medium-hot grill for 6–8 minutes on each side or until cooked through.

Serve immediately with a crisp green salad, rice or crusty bread.

 # Spicy Mango and Duck Salad

Serves 4

2 x 200g (7 oz) packs mango chunks

4 shop-bought ready-cooked, smoked duck breasts, skin removed and roughly shredded

8 tablespoons shop-bought mayonnaise

4 tablespoons sweet chilli sauce

juice of 1 lime

salt and pepper

- Put the mango and shredded duck in a large salad bowl and season well.

- Mix together the mayonnaise, sweet chilli sauce and lime juice in a bowl. Pour the dressing over the salad, toss to mix well and serve.

 ### Mango and Duck Curry

Heat 2 tablespoons sunflower oil in a large wok until hot, add 1 chopped onion, 1 deseeded and chopped red chilli, 1 chopped garlic clove and 1 teaspoon peeled and grated fresh root ginger and stir-fry for 1–2 minutes. Add 600 g (1 lb 5 oz) boneless, skinless duck breasts, cut into bite-sized pieces, and stir-fry over a high heat for 3–4 minutes until lightly golden. Stir in a 400 ml (14 fl oz) can coconut milk, 100 ml (3½ fl oz) water and 2 tablespoons medium curry paste and bring to the boil. Mix well and cook, uncovered, for 10–12 minutes or until the duck is cooked through. Stir in 2 x 200 g (7 oz) packs mango chunks and heat until warmed through. Remove from the heat and serve with steamed rice.

 ### Spicy Mango and Duck Noodles

Put 2 large skinless duck breasts, cut into thin strips, into a large bowl. Mix together 2 tablespoons sunflower oil, 2 tablespoons hot chilli sauce, 4 tablespoons sweet chilli sauce and 4 tablespoons soy sauce in a small bowl, then pour the mixture over the duck, season and toss to coat evenly. Cover and leave to marinate for 15 minutes. Heat a nonstick wok or frying pan until hot. Using a slotted spoon, add the duck to the wok, reserving the marinade, and stir-fry over a high heat for 5 minutes or until lightly golden and just cooked through. Add a 200 g (7 oz) pack mango chunks, a 300 g (10 oz) pack ready-prepared stir-fry vegetables, 2 x 300 g (10 oz) packs

ready-cooked medium egg noodles and the reserved marinade and stir-fry for a further few minutes until piping hot. Stir in 75 g (3 oz) dry-roasted peanuts, chopped. Divide into warm bowls and serve immediately.

20 Spicy Chicken, Mushroom and Spinach Pancakes

Serves 4

2 tablespoons butter, plus extra
  for greasing
300 g (10 oz) baby chestnut
  mushrooms, sliced
6 spring onions, finely sliced
2 garlic cloves, crushed
1 tablespoon hot curry powder
1 red chilli, deseeded and sliced
500 g (1 lb) pot four cheese sauce
300 g (10 oz) baby spinach leaves
2 shop-bought ready-cooked
  chicken breasts, skin removed
  and shredded
4 tablespoons chopped coriander
8 shop-bought savoury pancakes,
  thawed if frozen
50 g (2 oz) Parmesan cheese,
  grated
salt and pepper
mixed salad, to serve

• Heat the butter in a large frying pan, add the mushrooms, spring onions, garlic, curry powder and red chilli and cook over a high heat for 4–5 minutes, stirring frequently, until the mushrooms are softened. Stir in half of the cheese sauce and heat until just bubbling. Add the spinach and cook for 1 minute or until just wilted. Remove from the heat, stir in the chicken and coriander and season.

• Place 1 pancake on a clean work surface and spoon one-eighth of the mushroom and spinach mixture down the centre. Carefully roll the pancake up and put into a shallow greased gratin dish. Repeat with the remaining pancakes.

• Drizzle the remaining cheese sauce over the pancakes, sprinkle with the Parmesan and season to taste. Cook under a preheated medium-hot grill for 3–4 minutes or until piping hot and golden. Serve with a mixed salad.

---

10 Chicken, Mushroom and Spinach Salad with Spicy Yogurt Dressing

Put 4 shop-bought ready-cooked chicken breasts, skin removed and shredded, 200 g (7 oz) baby spinach leaves and 200 g (7 oz) thinly sliced button mushrooms in a salad bowl. Mix together 300 ml (½ pint) natural yogurt with 1 tablespoon mild curry powder, 2 tablespoons chopped coriander and the juice of 1 lemon in a bowl, then season. Drizzle over the salad, toss to mix well and serve.

30 Spiced Chicken, Mushroom and Spinach Pilau

Heat 2 tablespoons sunflower oil in a heavy-based saucepan, add 1 chopped onion, 1 deseeded and finely chopped red chilli, 2 teaspoons cumin seeds, 1 cinnamon stick, 1 bay leaf, 1 tablespoon medium or hot curry powder and 400 g (13 oz) boneless, skinless chicken breasts, diced, and cook, stirring, for 1–2 minutes until the chicken is lightly browned. Add 400 g (13 oz) basmati rice, 200 g (7 oz) chopped spinach leaves and 200 g (7 oz) sliced button mushrooms and season, then stir to mix well. Pour in 800 ml (1 pint 8 fl oz) hot vegetable stock and bring to the boil. Cover tightly, reduce the heat to low and cook, undisturbed, for 15–20 minutes or until the liquid is absorbed, the rice is tender and the chicken is cooked through. Remove from the heat and leave to stand for a few minutes before serving.

Chicken, Chilli and Rosemary Soup

Serves 4

2 garlic cloves, crushed

1 red chilli, deseeded and finely chopped, plus extra to garnish

2 tablespoons finely chopped fresh rosemary

2 x 400 g cans cream of chicken soup

crusty bread rolls, to serve

To garnish

chilli oil

finely chopped chives

- Pour the soup into a saucepan, stir in the garlic, chilli and rosemary and bring to the boil. Reduce the heat to medium and cook for a few minutes or until piping hot.

- Remove from the heat. Ladle into bowls, sprinkle with the chives and the remaining chopped chilli, to garnish, and drizzle with chilli oil. Serve immediately with crusty bread rolls.

 Creamy Chicken, Chilli and Rosemary Pasta Cook 350 g (11½ oz) dried penne in a large saucepan of salted boiling water according to the packet instructions until al dente. Meanwhile, heat 2 tablespoons olive oil in a large frying pan, add 2 chopped garlic cloves, 2 deseeded and finely chopped red chillies and 400 g (13 oz) boneless, skinless chicken thighs, chopped, and cook over a medium heat, stirring occasionally, for 8–10 minutes or until the chicken is sealed and cooked through. Add 1 teaspoon dried rosemary and 200 ml (7 fl oz) crème fraîche. Drain the pasta, add to the frying pan and season. Toss to mix well, then serve immediately with a rocket salad.

 Rosemary and Chilli-Stuffed Chicken Whizz 35 g (1½ oz) finely chopped flat leaf parsley, 2 tablespoons finely chopped rosemary, 2 deseeded and finely chopped red chillies, 2 tablespoons grated Pecorino cheese, 2 crushed garlic cloves, 1½ tablespoons softened unsalted butter and the finely grated rind and juice of 1 lemon to a paste in a food processor or blender, then season well. Take 4 large boneless chicken breasts, with skin on, and carefully lift the skin away from the breast meat, leaving it still attached at one end. Spoon the herb mixture on to the chicken breasts, then smooth the skin back down to cover the herb mixture. Heat 2 tablespoons olive oil and 1½ tablespoons butter in an ovenproof frying pan, add the chicken breasts, skin-side down, and carefully fry for 1–2 minutes or until the skin is crisp and golden brown. Turn the chicken over and cook for a further 1 minute. Transfer the pan to a preheated oven, 180°C (350°F), Gas Mark 4, and cook for 12–15 minutes or until the chicken is cooked through. Cover with foil and leave to rest for 5 minutes before serving with a mixed salad.

30 Curried Chicken and Peas

Serves 4

3 tablespoons vegetable oil

2 teaspoons cumin seeds

2 onions, finely chopped

1 tablespoon peeled and grated
   fresh root ginger

1 tablespoon grated garlic

500 g (1 lb) minced chicken

2 tablespoons ground coriander

1 teaspoon hot chilli powder

1 tablespoon ground cumin

1 tablespoon garam masala

1 red pepper, cored, deseeded and
   finely chopped

100 g (3½ oz) frozen peas

2 ripe tomatoes, finely chopped

juice of ½ lime

chopped coriander leaves,
   to garnish

To serve

warm chapatis or parathas

natural yogurt

- Heat the oil in a large wok or frying pan until hot, add the cumin seeds and stir-fry over a medium heat for 1 minute. Add the onions and stir-fry for a further 3–4 minutes until softened, then add the ginger and garlic and continue to stir-fry for 1 minute.

- Add the minced chicken and the ground spices and stir-fry for 5–7 minutes or until sealed and lightly browned. Stir in the red pepper, peas and tomatoes and stir-fry for a further 3–4 minutes or until cooked through and piping hot.

- Remove from the heat and stir in the lime juice. Spoon into warm bowls, scatter with chopped coriander and serve with warm chapatis or parathas and a dollop of yogurt.

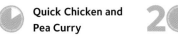

1 Quick Chicken and Pea Curry

Heat 2 tablespoons olive oil in a large wok until hot, add 600 g (1 lb 5 oz) minced chicken, 2 tablespoons green curry paste and stir-fry over a high heat for 3–4 minutes or until the chicken is cooked through. Stir in a 400 ml (14 fl oz) can coconut milk and 100 g (3½ oz) frozen peas and cook for a further 3–4 minutes. Season well, then serve with jasmine rice or crusty bread.

2 Spicy Chicken and Pea Bolognese

Heat 1 tablespoon olive oil in a saucepan, add 4 chopped shallots, 2 teaspoons cumin seeds, 4 crushed garlic cloves, 100 g (3½ oz) frozen peas, 1 teaspoon peeled and grated fresh root ginger, 1 teaspoon ground cumin, 1 teaspoon ground coriander and 1 teaspoon hot chilli powder and stir-fry over a high heat for 1–2 minutes. Add 500 g (1 lb) minced chicken and stir-fry for a further 2–3 minutes until lightly browned, then add a 400 g (13 oz) can chopped tomatoes, 100 ml (3½ fl oz) passata and 1 teaspoon sugar. Season, bring to the boil, then reduce the heat to medium and cook for 20 minutes. Serve with cooked pasta.

30 Chicken, Prawn and Lemon Grass Cakes

Serves 4

400 g (13 oz) minced chicken
400 g (13 oz) raw peeled tiger prawns
4 cm (1½ inch) length of trimmed lemon grass stalk, finely chopped
50 g (2 oz) chopped coriander
5 tablespoons chopped mint
1 tablespoon peeled and grated fresh root ginger
2 large garlic cloves, crushed
1 red chilli, deseeded and finely chopped
1 tablespoon medium curry powder
200 g (7 oz) dried rice noodles
2 tablespoons sunflower oil, for brushing
salt and pepper

To serve
lime wedges
sweet chilli dipping sauce

- Put the chicken, prawns, lemon grass, chopped herbs, ginger, garlic, red chilli and curry powder in a food processor or blender and blitz until fairly smooth. Using wet hands, divide the mixture into 12 portions and shape each portion into a cake. Transfer to a nonstick baking sheet, cover and chill for 8–10 minutes.

- Meanwhile, cook the rice noodles according to the packet instructions, then drain and keep warm.

- Brush the cakes with oil and season. Cook under a preheated medium-hot grill, turning once or twice, for about 10 minutes or until browned and just cooked through.

- Transfer the cakes on to 4 serving plates and serve with the rice noodles, lime wedges and a sweet chilli dipping sauce.

10 Chicken, Prawn and Lemon Grass Stir-Fry

Heat 2 tablespoons sunflower oil in a large wok or frying pan until hot, add 500 g (1 lb) minced chicken, 1 tablespoon green curry paste and 1 tablespoon lemon grass paste and stir-fry over a high heat for 3–4 minutes or until sealed and browned. Stir in 300 g (10 oz) cooked peeled prawns, 1 tablespoon light soy sauce and 1 tablespoon fish sauce and heat for 3–4 minutes until piping hot. Serve with noodles.

20 Chicken, Prawn and Lemon Grass Skewers

Place 400 g (13 oz) minced chicken, 400 g (13 oz) raw peeled tiger prawns, 1 tablespoon lemon grass paste, 1 teaspoon each ginger paste and garlic paste, 1 teaspoon sweet chilli sauce and 100 g (3½ oz) fresh white breadcrumbs in a food processor or blender and blitz until fairly smooth, then season. Divide into 12 portions, then shape each portion around a metal skewer into a long sausage shape and cook under a preheated medium-hot grill for 3–4 minutes on each side or until cooked through. Serve with a mixed salad.

Curried Chicken and Grape Salad

Serves 4

4 large shop-bought ready-cooked chicken breasts, skin-on, cut into bite-sized pieces
large handful Baby Gem lettuce leaves
200 g (7 oz) cherry tomatoes, halved
200 g (7 oz) seedless green grapes, halved
6 spring onions, thinly sliced

For the curry mayonnaise

200 ml (7 fl oz) mayonnaise
2 teaspoons medium or hot curry powder
finely grated rind and juice of 1 lemon
20 g (¾ oz) coriander leaves, finely chopped

- To make the curry mayonnaise, put all the ingredients in a bowl and stir to mix well. Set aside.

- Put the chicken breasts, lettuce leaves, tomatoes, grapes and spring onions in a large salad bowl and mix well.

- Spoon over the mayonnaise, toss to mix well and serve with crusty bread, if liked.

Curried Chicken Pasta Salad

Cook 250 g (8 oz) dried penne in a large saucepan of salted boiling water according to the packet instructions until al dente. Meanwhile, put 4 shop-bought ready-cooked chicken breasts, skin removed and cut into bite-sized pieces, 1 diced cucumber, 200 g (7 oz) halved cherry tomatoes, 1 finely diced red onion and 1 diced dessert apple in a large salad bowl. Mix together 300 ml (½ pint) mayonnaise, 2 teaspoons medium-hot curry powder, the juice of 2 limes, 1 teaspoon runny honey, 2 teaspoons toasted cumin seeds and a small handful of finely chopped coriander leaves in a bowl, then season and stir to mix well. Drain the pasta, then add to the chicken mixture. Pour over the dressing, toss to mix well and serve warm or at room temperature.

Grilled Chicken with Curry Mayonnaise

Make the curry mayonnaise as above. Put 4 large boneless, skinless chicken breasts in a bowl. Mix 6 tablespoons olive oil, 1 teaspoon dried red chilli flakes, 2 teaspoons paprika, 2 crushed garlic cloves and the grated rind and juice of 1 lemon in a bowl, then season. Pour the mixture over the chicken and toss. Cook under a preheated medium-hot grill for 6–8 minutes on each side or until cooked through. Cover and leave to rest for 2–3 minutes. Serve with the curry mayonnaise and salad.

30 Duck Tikka Kebabs

Serves 4

4 large skinless duck breasts, cut
  into bite-sized pieces
200 ml (7 fl oz) natural yogurt
3 tablespoons tikka paste
1 tablespoon finely grated garlic
1 tablespoon peeled and finely
  grated fresh root ginger
juice of 2 limes
2 red peppers, cored, deseeded
  and cut into bite-sized pieces
salt and pepper
chopped coriander leaves,
  to garnish

To serve

steamed rice
chopped cucumber salad

- Put the duck in a large non-reactive bowl. Mix together the yogurt, tikka paste, garlic, ginger and lime juice in a small bowl, then season. Pour the mixture over the duck and toss to coat evenly, then cover and leave to marinate for 10 minutes.

- Thread the duck on to 8 metal skewers, alternating with the red peppers. Cook under a preheated medium-hot grill for 5–6 minutes on each side or until the edges are lightly charred in places and the duck is just cooked through (it should still be a little pink in the centre).

- Transfer the skewers on to 4 serving plates and serve with steamed rice and a chopped cucumber salad.

 Duck and Vegetable Tikka Stir-Fry

Heat 1 tablespoon sunflower oil in a large wok or frying pan until hot, add 1 tablespoon tikka paste, 8 sliced spring onions and a 400 g (13 oz) pack ready-prepared stir-fry vegetables and stir-fry over a high heat for 3–4 minutes until softened. Add 2 shop-bought smoked duck breasts, sliced, 3 tablespoons sweet chilli sauce and 2 tablespoons soy sauce and stir-fry for a further 4–5 minutes or until piping hot. Serve immediately with steamed rice.

 Tikka-Spiced Duck Omelette

Heat 2 tablespoons sunflower oil in a medium ovenproof frying pan, add 6 sliced spring onions, 2 chopped garlic cloves and 1 deseeded and finely chopped red chilli and cook over a high heat, stirring, for 1–2 minutes until softened. Add 1 tablespoon tikka paste and 2 finely diced smoked duck breasts and cook for a further 1–2 minutes. Meanwhile, whisk together 6 eggs and 4 tablespoons chopped coriander leaves in a bowl, then season and pour into the pan. Cook over a medium heat for 10–12 minutes or until the base is set, then place the pan under a preheated medium-hot grill and cook for 4–5 minutes or until the top is golden and set. Serve warm or at room temperature.

30 Chinese Turkey Chow Mein

Serves 4

3 turkey breast fillets, thinly sliced
4 tablespoons light soy sauce
1 tablespoon hot chilli sauce
2 teaspoons white wine vinegar
4 garlic cloves, crushed
2 teaspoons peeled and finely
   grated fresh root ginger
1 teaspoon 5-spice powder
200 g (7 oz) dried egg noodles
2 tablespoons vegetable oil
200 g (7 oz) mangetout, halved
200 g (7 oz) canned water
   chestnuts, drained
100 g (3½ oz) canned bamboo
   shoots, drained
1 red pepper, cored, deseeded and
   thinly sliced
8 spring onions, sliced diagonally
3 tablespoons oyster sauce
2 tablespoons sweet chilli sauce
2 tablespoons dark soy sauce
½ teaspoon toasted sesame oil

- Put the turkey in a shallow non-reactive bowl. Mix together the light soy sauce, hot chilli sauce, vinegar, garlic, ginger and 5-spice powder in a bowl. Pour over the turkey and toss to coat evenly, then cover and leave to marinate for 10 minutes.

- Meanwhile, cook the noodles according to the packet instructions, then drain.

- Heat the vegetable oil in a large wok or frying pan until hot, add the turkey mixture and stir-fry over a high heat for 4–5 minutes until lightly browned. Add all the vegetables and stir-fry for a further 4–5 minutes, then add the drained noodles, oyster sauce, sweet chilli sauce, dark soy sauce and sesame oil and toss together for 4 minutes or until piping hot and the turkey is cooked through.

- Divide into warm bowls and serve immediately.

 Chinese Turkey and Noodle Salad

Cook 300 g (10 oz) dried medium egg noodles according to the packet instructions, drain and refresh under cold running water, then drain again. Put the noodles, 400 g (13 oz) shop-bought ready-cooked sliced turkey breast, ½ cucumber, thinly shredded, and ½ carrot, peeled and thinly shredded, in a large salad bowl, then add 2 sliced spring onions. Mix together 2 tablespoons sweet chilli sauce, 2 tablespoons light soy sauce, 1 teaspoon hot chilli sauce and 3 tablespoons rice wine vinegar in a bowl. Drizzle the dressing over the salad, toss to mix well and serve.

2 Glazed Chinese-Style Turkey Steaks

Put 4 turkey breast steaks in a dish. Mix 1 tablespoon hot chilli sauce, 2 tablespoons sweet chilli sauce, 2 tablespoons light soy sauce and 1 tablespoon oyster sauce in a bowl. Spread over the turkey, cover and leave to marinate for 5–10 minutes. Cook under a preheated medium-hot grill for 3–4 minutes on each side or until the turkey is cooked through. Serve with rice.

QuickCook
Meat

Recipes listed by cooking time

30

20

10

30 African Curried Beef and Mango Chutney Bake

Serves 4

2 tablespoons sunflower oil
500 g (1lb) minced beef
1 large onion, finely chopped
2 garlic cloves, crushed
2 tablespoons medium
  curry powder
4 tablespoons mango chutney
100 g (3½ oz) fresh white
  breadcrumbs
200 ml (7 fl oz) Greek yogurt
3 large eggs
salt and pepper
chopped coriander leaves,
  to garnish
leafy green salad, to serve

- Heat the oil in a large wok or frying pan until hot, add the beef and stir-fry over a high heat for 2–3 minutes until browned. Add the onion, garlic and curry powder and stir-fry for a further 1–2 minutes until beginning to soften.

- Remove from the heat, stir in the mango chutney and breadcrumbs and toss to mix well. Spoon the mixture into a shallow ovenproof dish.

- Whisk together the yogurt and eggs in a bowl and season well, then pour over the beef mixture. Cook in a preheated oven, 200°C (400°F), Gas Mark 6, for 20–25 minutes or until piping hot and the top is set and golden brown.

- Scatter with chopped coriander and serve with a leafy green salad.

 Curried Beef and Mango Chutney Rolls Halve 4 warm bread rolls, then spread each half with 1 tablespoon mayonnaise and lightly sprinkle over a little medium curry powder. Top each base with 1 tablespoon mango chutney and 3–4 thin slices of shop-bought ready-cooked roast beef. Sandwich with the lids and serve.

 Curried Beef and Mango Chutney Wraps Heat 2 tablespoons sunflower oil in a large frying pan, add 300 g (10 oz) minced beef, 1 teaspoon ginger paste, 1 teaspoon garlic paste and 1 tablespoon medium curry paste and cook, stirring, over a medium heat for 5–6 minutes or until browned and cooked through. Add 2 chopped tomatoes and 4 sliced spring onions and cook for a further 2–3 minutes. Season, remove from the heat and stir in 3 tablespoons mango chutney. Warm 8 large flatbreads in a griddle pan or dry frying pan according to the packet instructions, then spread each with 1 tablespoon natural yogurt. Divide the beef mixture between the flatbreads, roll up to form wraps and serve immediately.

30 Chinese Beef with Tofu and Vegetables

Serves 4

2 tablespoons sunflower oil

400 g (13 oz) firm tofu, cut into 2 cm (¾ inch) cubes

2 teaspoons grated fresh root ginger

6 spring onions, chopped, plus extra, to garnish

1 red chilli, deseeded and finely chopped, plus extra, to garnish

½ red pepper, cored, deseeded and cut into thick strips

½ yellow pepper, cored, deseeded and cut into thick strips

200 g (7 oz) sliced shiitake mushrooms

1 tablespoon cornflour

2 tablespoons dark soy sauce

2 tablespoons oyster sauce

50 ml (2 fl oz) mirin

200 ml (7 fl oz) hot vegetable stock

400 g (13 oz) ready-cooked roast beef slices, cut into strips

steamed rice, to serve

- Heat the oil in a wok until hot, add the tofu in batches and stir-fry over a high heat for 3–4 minutes or until golden. Remove with a slotted spoon and drain on kitchen paper.

- Add the ginger, spring onions, red chilli, red and yellow peppers and mushrooms to the wok and stir-fry over a high heat for 3–4 minutes until softened.

- Mix the cornflour with 2 tablespoons of water in a small bowl. Add the soy sauce, oyster sauce, mirin and stock, and mix well. Add the liquid to the wok and bring to the boil. Reduce the heat to medium-low, return the tofu to the wok with the beef strips, toss to mix well and simmer gently for 2–3 minutes until heated through.

- Ladle into warm bowls, scatter with sliced spring onion and red chilli and serve with steamed rice.

10 Chinese Beef, Tofu and Vegetable Salad

Core, deseed and slice 1 red pepper and 1 yellow pepper, then put in a large salad bowl with 400 g (13 oz) shop-bought ready-cooked roast beef slices, thickly sliced, 6 sliced spring onions and 200 g (7 oz) firm tofu, cubed. Mix 1 teaspoon ginger paste, 1 teaspoon chilli oil, 1 teaspoon sesame oil, 4 tablespoons sunflower oil and 6 tablespoons light soy sauce in a bowl. Stir to mix well, pour the dressing over the salad and serve.

20 Chinese Beef, Tofu and Vegetable

Noodles Heat 2 tablespoons sunflower oil in a large wok or frying pan until hot, add 400 g (13 oz) beef fillet, cut into thin strips, and stir-fry over a high heat for 3–4 minutes until browned. Add 8 sliced spring onions, 1 cored, deseeded and thinly sliced red pepper, 1 cored, deseeded and thinly sliced yellow pepper and 200 g (7 oz) very thinly sliced shiitake mushrooms and stir-fry for a further 4–5 minutes. Add 125 g (4 oz) shop-bought fresh Chinese stir-fry sauce, a 300g bag fresh rice noodles and 200 g (7 oz) firm tofu, cubed, and continue to stir-fry for 2–3 minutes or until piping hot. Serve immediately.

HOT-MEAT-LUE

30 Burmese Lemon Grass and Chilli Pork

Serves 4

1 tablespoon sesame oil

2 tablespoons vegetable oil

500 g (1lb) pork tenderloin, cut into bite-sized pieces

8 cm (3 inch) length of trimmed lemon grass stalk, finely chopped

2 tablespoons tamarind paste

1 tablespoon fish sauce

200 ml (7 fl oz) hot water

chopped coriander leaves, to garnish

steamed rice, to serve

For the spice paste

1 large onion, roughly chopped

2 garlic cloves, chopped

1 teaspoon peeled and finely grated fresh root ginger

1 teaspoon ground turmeric

1 red chilli, deseeded and finely chopped

1 teaspoon chilli powder

- To make the spice paste, put all the ingredients in a food processor or blender and blend to a paste, adding a little water if needed.

- Heat the oils in a wok or frying pan until hot, add the spice paste and stir-fry over a medium-high heat for 1–2 minutes. Add the pork and stir to mix well, then increase the heat to high and stir-fry for a further 8–10 minutes.

- Add the lemon grass, tamarind paste, fish sauce and measurement water and stir well. Cook for 3–4 minutes or until the pork is cooked through.

- Scatter with chopped coriander leaves and serve with steamed rice.

 Pork, Lemon Grass and Chilli Stir-Fry
Heat 2 tablespoons sunflower oil in a large wok or frying pan until hot, add 8 sliced spring onions, 300 g (10 oz) pork fillet, cut into very thin strips, and 1 deseeded and sliced red chilli and stir-fry over a high heat for 3–4 minutes until the pork is browned. Add 1 tablespoon lemon grass paste and 4 tablespoons light soy sauce and stir-fry for a further 1–2 minutes or until the pork is cooked through. Serve immediately with noodles or steamed rice.

 Pork Chops with Lemon Grass and Chilli Mix together 1 tablespoon lemon grass paste, 1 teaspoon ginger paste, 1 teaspoon garlic paste, 1 teaspoon chilli paste and 1 teaspoon tamarind paste in a bowl. Stir in 2 teaspoons runny honey, then spread the mixture all over 4 pork chops, about 200 g (7 oz) each, and season. Cook under a preheated hot grill for 5–6 minutes on each side or until just cooked through. Serve with a green salad.

Curried Calves' Liver with Herby Salad

Serves 4

2 Baby Gem lettuces
4 plum tomatoes
large handful of coriander leaves
large handful of mint leaves
450 g (14½ oz) calves' liver, trimmed
1 tablespoon medium curry powder
1 teaspoon ground cumin
1 teaspoon ground coriander
1 teaspoon crushed fennel seeds
½ teaspoon chilli powder
1 teaspoon minced garlic
1 teaspoon peeled and finely
  grated fresh root ginger
2 tablespoons white wine vinegar
4 tablespoons vegetable oil
salt and pepper
pinch of paprika, to garnish
lemon wedges, to serve

- Roughly shred the lettuce leaves, and chop the tomatoes. Place in a bowl with the coriander and mint, lightly toss together, then set aside.

- Put the liver in a separate bowl. Mix together the curry powder, cumin, ground coriander, fennel seeds, chilli powder, garlic, ginger and vinegar to make a smooth paste. Season well, then spread the mixture all over the liver.

- Heat the oil in a large frying pan over a high heat. Add the liver and cook, in batches if necessary, stirring, for 3–4 minutes until the liver is lightly browned but still slightly pink on the inside, then thickly slice.

- Divide the salad on to plates, top with the curried liver slices and sprinkle over the paprika. Serve with lemon wedges for squeezing over.

 Warm Curried Calves' Liver Salad

Heat 2 tablespoons sunflower oil in a frying pan, add 300 g (10 oz) sliced calves liver and fry for 2–3 minutes or until just sealed. Put in a salad bowl with 1 teaspoon ground cumin, ½ teaspoon chilli powder, 1 teaspoon crushed fennel seeds, 1 teaspoon finely chopped garlic, a handful each of chopped mint and coriander leaves and the torn leaves of 2 Baby Gem lettuces. Drizzle over 2 tablespoons olive oil and the juice of 1 lemon. Toss to mix well, season with salt and serve with crusty bread.

Curried Calves' Liver with Caramelized Onions

Heat 2 tablespoons sunflower oil in large frying pan, add 3 thinly sliced onions and cook over a low heat for 15–20 minutes or until lightly caramelized and golden. Season, then set aside. Meanwhile, cut 500 g (1 lb) trimmed calves liver into bite-sized pieces and sprinkle over 2 tablespoons mild curry powder. Season with salt and toss to mix well. Wipe out the pan, add 50 g (2 oz) butter and heat until foaming. Add the seasoned liver and cook, stirring, for 40–50 seconds. Return the onions to the pan, then cook for a further 1–2 minutes until the liver is just cooked through. Remove from the heat, then stir in the juice of 1 lemon and a small handful of chopped coriander. Serve with warm crusty rolls or naan bread.

Grilled Tandoori Lamb Chops

Serves 4

8 lamb loin chops or cutlets
3 garlic cloves, finely grated
1 teaspoon peeled and finely
  grated fresh root ginger
juice of 2 large lemons
1 tablespoon ground cumin
3 tablespoons tandoori
  curry paste
250 ml (8 fl oz) natural yogurt
salt and pepper
chopped mint leaves, to garnish

To serve

cucumber salad
mini naan breads

- Put the lamb in a single layer in a shallow non-reactive dish. Mix together the remaining ingredients in a bowl, then season well. Pour the mixture over the lamb, toss to coat evenly, then cover and leave to marinate for 10 minutes.

- Place the lamb on a lightly oiled grill rack and cook under a preheated hot grill for 2–3 minutes on each side or until cooked to your liking.

- Transfer on to 4 warm serving plates, scatter with chopped mint and serve with cucumber salad and mini naan breads.

Tandoori Lamb Wraps

Prepare and cook the lamb chops as above, omitting the marinating time. Meanwhile, warm 4 flatbreads in a griddle pan or dry frying pan according to the packet instructions, then spread with mayonnaise. Divide 2 sliced tomatoes, ½ sliced red onion and ¼ sliced cucumber between the flatbreads, then top with the finely sliced cooked lamb chops. Roll up the flatbreads to form wraps and serve immediately.

Tandoori Roast Rack of Lamb

Mix together 3 tablespoons tandoori paste and 100 ml (3½ fl oz) Greek yogurt in a bowl. Using a small, sharp knife, make deep slashes in the meat of 2 French-trimmed racks of lamb (with about 7–8 ribs each). Season well, then spread the tandoori paste all over the lamb. Put the racks, rib-side up, on a nonstick baking sheet and place in a preheated oven, 180°C (350°F), Gas Mark 4, for 15–20 minutes or until cooked to your liking. Cover with foil and leave to rest for a few minutes before serving.

Hot and Spicy Steak and Rocket Ciabattas

Serves 4

2 large sirloin steaks
olive oil, for brushing
2 large ciabatta loaves
2 tablespoons chilli sauce
100 g (3½ oz) shop-bought
 garlic mayonnaise
small handful of wild
 rocket leaves
salt and pepper

- Season the steaks and brush with a little oil. Place on a preheated smoking-hot ridged griddle pan and cook for 2–3 minutes on each side or until cooked to your liking.

- Meanwhile, put the ciabatta loaves on a baking sheet and place in a preheated oven, 200°C (400°F), Gas Mark 6, for 4–5 minutes or until warmed through.

- Mix together the chilli sauce and garlic mayonnaise in a bowl. Split the ciabatta loaves into half horizontally, spread the halves with the spicy mayonnaise and top the bases with some rocket leaves.

- Thinly slice the steaks, divide between the bases and top with the ciabatta lids. Cut each ciabatta into 2 and serve.

20 Spicy Steak, Potato and Rocket Salad

Cook 400 g (13 oz) baby new potatoes in a large saucepan of boiling water for 12–15 minutes or until just tender. Meanwhile, mix together 100 g (3½ oz) shop-bought garlic mayonnaise, 2 tablespoons hot chilli sauce, the juice of 1 lemon, 200 g (7 oz) natural yogurt, 6 tablespoons finely chopped chives and 6 tablespoons finely chopped dill in a bowl. Season and set aside. Place 2 large sirloin steaks on a preheated smoking-hot griddle pan and cook for 2–3 minutes on each side or until cooked to your liking, then cut into thin strips. Drain the potatoes, then halve and put in a large salad bowl with 100 g (3½ oz) wild rocket leaves and the steak strips. Pour the spicy dressing over the salad, toss to mix well and serve.

30 Spicy Spaghetti Bolognese

Heat 1 tablespoon olive oil in a pan. Add 1 chopped onion, 3 chopped garlic cloves, 2 chopped red chillies and 450 g (14½ oz) steak mince. Stir-fry over a high heat for 1–2 minutes, then stir in a 400 g (13 oz) can chopped tomatoes and 200 ml (7 fl oz) beef stock. Season and bring to a boil. Cook, uncovered, over a medium heat for 20 minutes, stirring occasionally. Meanwhile, cook 375 g (12 oz) spaghetti in a large saucepan of salted water according to the packet instructions. Drain and divide between 4 warmed pasta bowls. Spoon over the Bolognese and serve with a wild rocket salad.

HOT-MEAT-QUL

Lamb Chops with Spicy Chickpeas and Spinach

Serves 4

2 tablespoons olive oil

8 lamb chops, about 150 g
(5 oz) each

2 x 400 g (13 oz) cans chickpeas,
drained and rinsed

2 red chillies, deseeded and
finely chopped

2 teaspoons cumin seeds

1 teaspoon crushed coriander
seeds

100 g (3½ oz) roasted red
peppers from a jar, drained
and sliced

finely grated rind and juice of
1 lemon

400 g (13 oz) baby spinach leaves

small handful of coriander leaves,
chopped, plus extra to garnish

salt and pepper

- Heat the oil in a large frying pan, add the chops, in batches if necessary, and cook over a medium heat for 2–3 minutes on each side or until cooked to your liking. Remove from the pan, cover with foil and keep warm.

- Add the remaining ingredients to the pan, increase the heat to high and cook, stirring, for 4–5 minutes or until piping hot and the spinach has wilted.

- Spoon the chickpea mixture into 4 warm bowls and season to taste. Top with the lamb chops, scatter with extra chopped coriander and serve immediately.

10 Spicy Lamb, Spinach and Chickpea Salad

Brush 4 lamb leg steaks, about 150 g (5 oz) each, with 1 tablespoon olive oil, then cook under a preheated hot grill for 2–3 minutes on each side or until cooked to your liking. Meanwhile, put 100 g (3½ oz) baby spinach leaves, 2 chopped tomatoes and a rinsed and drained 400 g (13 oz) can chickpeas in a large salad bowl. Cut the slightly cooled lamb into bite-sized pieces and add to the bowl. Pour over 150 ml (¼ pint) shop-bought fresh vinaigrette, then sprinkle over 1 teaspoon hot curry powder and season. Toss to mix well and serve.

30 Spicy Lamb, Spinach and Chickpea Rice

Cook the Lamb Chops with Spicy Chickpeas and Spinach as above. Using a sharp knife, cut the meat from the cooked chops and cut into strips. Heat 1 tablespoon olive oil in a large frying pan until hot, add the cooked chickpea mixture and 250 g (8 oz) shop-bought ready-cooked basmati rice and stir-fry over a high heat for 4–5 minutes. Stir in the lamb and 100 ml (3½ fl oz) hot vegetable stock and cook for 2–3 minutes or until piping hot. Serve immediately.

30 Pork, Red Pepper and Pea Curry

Serves 4

3 tablespoons vegetable oil

2 teaspoons cumin seeds

2 onions, finely chopped

1 tablespoon peeled and grated
fresh root ginger

1 tablespoon grated garlic

500 g (1 lb) minced pork

2 tablespoons ground coriander

1 tablespoon ground cumin

1 tablespoon garam masala

1 red pepper, deseeded and
finely chopped

100 g (3½ oz) frozen peas

2 ripe tomatoes, finely chopped

juice of ½ lime

salt

chopped coriander leaves,
to garnish

To serve

natural yogurt

warm parathas or chapattis
(optional)

- Heat the oil in a large wok or frying pan until hot, add the cumin seeds and stir-fry over a medium heat for 1 minute, then add the onions and stir-fry for a further 3–4 minutes until softened. Add the ginger and garlic and continue to stir-fry for 1 minute.

- Add the pork and all the ground spices, season with salt and stir-fry for 8–10 minutes or until the pork is browned and cooked through. Stir in the red pepper, peas and tomatoes and stir-fry for a further 3–4 minutes or until the vegetables are tender. Remove from the heat and stir in the lime juice.

- Scatter with chopped coriander and serve with a dollop of yogurt and warm parathas or chapattis, if liked.

 Vietnamese Style Pork Baguettes

Prepare the cooked pork mixture as above. Meanwhile, split 2 warmed baguettes in half lengthways. Divide the cooked pork between the cut sides of the 2 baguettes. Top with 2 sliced tomatoes and a small handful of fresh mint and coriander leaves. Top with the baguette lids and serve.

 Curried Pork Chops

Mix together 2 teaspoons ginger paste, 2 teaspoons garlic paste, 1 tablespoon ground coriander, 2 teaspoons ground cumin, the juice of 1 lime and 2 tablespoons sunflower oil in a bowl, then spread the mixture all over 4 pork chops, about 200 g (7 oz) each, and season. Cover and leave to marinate for 5 minutes. Cook under a preheated hot grill for 5–6 minutes on each side or until cooked through. Serve with a crisp green salad.

30 Chorizo Sausage, Paprika and Bean Stew

Serves 4

2 tablespoons olive oil

200 g (7 oz) bacon lardons

500 g (8 oz) mini cooking Spanish
chorizo sausages

1 onion, finely chopped

3 x 400 g (13 oz) cans chopped
tomatoes with herbs

1 teaspoon caster sugar

1 tablespoon sweet smoked paprika

2 garlic cloves, crushed

1 carrot, peeled and finely diced

1 celery stick, finely diced

1 bay leaf

1 chicken stock cube, crumbled

2 x 400 g (13 oz) cans mixed beans,
such as black-eyed beans and red
kidney beans, rinsed and drained

4 tablespoons finely chopped flat
leaf parsley, plus extra to garnish

salt and pepper

crusty bread, to serve (optional)

- Heat the oil in a large heavy-based saucepan, add the bacon and chorizo sausages and cook over a high heat for 3–4 minutes until golden brown.

- Stir in the onion, tomatoes, sugar, paprika, garlic, carrot, celery, bay leaf and crumbled stock cube, then reduce the heat to medium and cook, uncovered, for 15–20 minutes.

- Stir in the beans and bring back to the boil, then cook for 2–3 minutes or until piping hot. Season and stir in the parsley.

- Ladle into warm bowls, scatter with extra chopped parsley and serve with crusty bread, if liked.

 Quick Chorizo, Paprika and Bean Soup Heat 1 tablespoon olive oil in a large saucepan, add 200 g (7 oz) diced chorizo and cook over a high heat for 2–3 minutes. Stir in 1 teaspoon sweet smoked paprika, then add a 600 g (1 lb 5 oz) pot fresh tomato soup and a rinsed and drained 400 g (13 oz) can mixed beans. Bring to the boil, then reduce the heat to medium and cook for 3–4 minutes or until piping hot. Serve with crusty bread.

 Pan-Fried Chorizo, Paprika and Beans Heat 1 tablespoon olive oil in a large frying pan, add 500 g (1 lb) cooking chorizo, thinly sliced, and cook, stirring, over a high heat for 4–5 minutes until golden brown. Add 1 chopped onion, 2 chopped garlic cloves and 2 teaspoons sweet smoked paprika and cook for a further 4–5 minutes until softened, then add 2 rinsed and drained 400 g (13 oz) cans mixed beans.

Season, then heat through until piping hot and serve with warmed tortillas, soured cream and guacamole.

10 Beef and Mixed Peppercorn Stroganoff

Serves 4

2 tablespoons butter

1 red onion, thinly sliced

250 g (8 oz) button mushrooms, halved

3 tablespoons tomato purée

2 teaspoons Dijon mustard

1 tablespoon pink peppercorns in brine, drained

1 tablespoon green peppercorns in brine, drained

1 teaspoon smoked paprika

300 ml (½ pint) hot beef stock

500 g (1 lb) beef fillet, cut into thin strips

200 ml (7 fl oz) soured cream

salt and pepper

2 tablespoons chopped flat leaf parsley, to garnish

steamed rice, to serve

- Heat a frying pan until hot, then add half the butter. When foaming, add the red onion and fry for 2–3 minutes or until just softened. Add the mushrooms, tomato purée, mustard, pink and green peppercorns and paprika and fry, stirring, for a further 1–2 minutes. Pour in the beef stock and bring to the boil, then reduce the heat to low and simmer for 1–2 minutes.

- Meanwhile, heat a separate frying pan and add the remaining butter. Season the beef. When the butter is foaming, add the beef and cook, stirring, for 2–3 minutes or until browned all over.

- Add the soured cream and beef to the onion and mushroom mixture and mix well, then season to taste.

- Spoon into warm bowls, scatter over the parsley and serve with steamed rice.

---

 20 Cheat's Spiced Beef and Mushroom Pie Use the cooked beef and mushroom mixture from the above recipe to fill 4 individual pie dishes. Top each with 200g ready-cooked mashed potato and place under a hot grill for 3–4 minutes or until golden. Serve with a salad.

30 Beef and Mixed Peppercorn Pilau Heat 1 tablespoon butter and 1 tablespoon sunflower oil in a heavy-based saucepan, add 1 chopped onion and 400 g (13 oz) minced beef and cook, stirring, over a high heat for 3–4 minutes until the onion is softened and the beef is browned. Add 1 tablespoon drained pink peppercorns in brine, 1 tablespoon drained green peppercorns in brine, 2 crushed garlic cloves, 4 tablespoons tomato purée, 200 g (7 oz) baby button mushrooms and 350 g (11½ oz) basmati rice and stir until well coated, then pour in 800 ml (1 pint 8 fl oz) hot beef stock, season and bring to the boil. Cover tightly, reduce the heat to medium-low and cook gently, undisturbed, for 15–20 minutes or until the rice is tender. Remove from the heat and leave to stand for a few minutes before serving.

30 Spicy Beef Koftas with Mint Relish

Serves 4

600 g (1 lb 5 oz) minced beef
1 red onion, finely chopped
2 garlic cloves, crushed
1 red chilli, deseeded and chopped
small handful of mint, chopped
small handful of coriander, chopped
1 teaspoon ground ginger
1 teaspoon mild chilli powder
1 teaspoon ground cumin
2 teaspoons crushed coriander seeds
1 egg, beaten
100 g (3½ oz) fresh white
    breadcrumbs
2 tablespoons sunflower oil
salt and pepper
lime wedges, to serve

For the mint relish

1 onion, finely chopped
2 tomatoes, finely chopped
½ cucumber, finely chopped
150 g (5 oz) natural yogurt
4 tablespoons chopped mint leaves
2 tablespoons mint jelly
juice of 1 lime

- To make the mint relish, mix together all the ingredients in a bowl, cover and chill until needed.

- Put the beef, red onion, garlic, red chilli and herbs in a food processor or blender. Add the ground ginger, chilli powder, cumin, coriander seeds and egg. Season well, then process until fairly smooth and well combined.

- Divide the mixture into 16 balls. Roll each ball in the breadcrumbs, place on a baking sheet and drizzle with the oil. Place in a preheated oven, 200°C (400°F), Gas Mark 6, for 15–20 minutes or until cooked through.

- Serve the beef koftas on cocktail sticks with the mint relish and lime wedges to squeeze over.

---

10 Spicy Meatball Sarnies

Halve 4 ciabatta rolls and spread the bases with mayonnaise. Top each with a small handful of shredded iceberg lettuce, then divide a 350 g (11½ oz) pack ready-cooked meatballs between the bases. Squeeze over some chilli ketchup and top with the ciabatta lids. Serve with a salad.

20 Beef Kofta Curry

Put 600 g (1 lb 5 oz) minced beef, 1 tablespoon ginger paste, 1 tablespoon garlic paste, 1 deseeded and chopped red chilli and 1 tablespoon medium curry powder in a blender, then season and blend until well combined. Divide the mixture into bite-sized balls. Heat 2 tablespoons sunflower oil in a large frying pan, add the balls and cook over a medium heat for 2–3 minutes until browned. Stir in 300 ml (½ pint) hot beef stock, 1 tablespoon medium curry paste and 200 ml (7 fl oz) canned coconut milk. Bring to the boil, then cook, uncovered, for 8–10 minutes or until the koftas are cooked through and piping hot. Serve with steamed rice.

30 Spicy Chilli Dogs

Serves 4

12 good-quality pork sausages
4 tablespoons sweet chilli sauce
8 tablespoons tomato ketchup
2 teaspoons hot chilli sauce
4 tablespoons hoisin sauce
2 tablespoons runny honey
2 teaspoons Dijon or English
  mustard

To serve

12 split hot dog rolls
12 Baby Gem lettuce leaves

- Put the sausages in a roasting tin and insert a metal skewer through each lengthways. Mix together the remaining ingredients in a bowl, pour over the sausages and toss to mix well.

- Place in a preheated oven, 200°C (400°F), Gas Mark 6, for 20–25 minutes or until golden and cooked through.

- To serve, place 1 lettuce leaf in each of the hot dog rolls. Carefully remove the skewers from the sausages and serve in the rolls.

 Spicy Sausage Salad

Slice a 400 g (13 oz) pack ready-cooked cocktail sausages lengthways and put in a large salad bowl with 1 deseeded and finely chopped red chilli, 2 sliced tomatoes, 1 sliced cucumber and a 100 g (3½ oz) bag mixed salad leaves. Drizzle 150 ml (¼ pint) shop-bought fresh salad dressing over the salad, season and toss to mix well. Serve with warm rolls.

 Spicy Sausage and Bean Stew

Heat 2 tablespoons sunflower oil in a heavy-based saucepan, add 12 roughly chopped thick pork sausages, 1 chopped onion, 1 teaspoon ginger paste, 1 teaspoon garlic paste and 1 teaspoon chilli paste and cook over a high heat for 3–4 minutes until the sausages are browned. Stir in 3 x 400 g (13 oz) cans baked beans and 2 tablespoons tomato purée and bring to the boil, then reduce the heat to medium and cook, uncovered, for 8–10 minutes or until the sausages are cooked through. Season, then stir in a small handful of flat leaf parsley, chopped, and serve with baked potatoes.

20 Spicy Lamb and Herb Kebabs

Serves 4

4 garlic cloves, crushed
3 red chillies, deseeded and chopped
1 tablespoon ground coriander
2 tablespoons ground cumin
¼ red pepper, cored, deseeded and finely diced
¼ yellow pepper, cored, deseeded and finely diced
½ small onion, finely chopped
15 g (½ oz) chopped mint leaves
15 g (½ oz) chopped flat leaf parsley
600 g (1 lb 5 oz) minced lamb
4 tablespoons natural yogurt
olive oil, for brushing
sumac, for sprinkling
¼ iceberg lettuce, shredded
2 plum tomatoes, thinly sliced
¼ cucumber, halved and sliced
½ red onion, thinly sliced
juice of 2 limes, plus wedges, to serve
salt and pepper

- To make the kebabs, put the garlic, red chillies, ground spices, peppers, onion, mint, herbs and lamb in a mixing bowl and season well. Using your hands, combine thoroughly until well mixed. Cover and leave to marinate for 10 minutes to allow the flavours to develop.

- Divide the lamb mixture into 12 portions, then shape each portion around a metal skewer into a long sausage shape. Place on a grill rack, lightly brush with olive oil and sprinkle the kebabs with a little sumac. Cook under a preheated medium-hot grill for 4–5 minutes on each side or until cooked through.

- Meanwhile, make the salad by mixing the lettuce, tomatoes, cucumber, red onion and lime juice in a bowl and season well.

- Serve the kebabs with the salad and lime wedges to squeeze over.

10 Spicy Lamb Stir-Fry

Heat 2 tablespoons olive oil in a large wok until hot, add 1 chopped onion, 2 deseeded and sliced red chillies, 2 teaspoons ground cumin, 1 teaspoon ground cinnamon and 600 g (1 lb 5 oz) minced lamb and stir-fry over a high heat for 6–8 minutes or until the lamb is cooked through. Stir in 4 tablespoons each of chopped coriander and mint leaves. Serve immediately with crusty bread.

30 Spiced Lamb Pilau

Heat 2 tablespoons olive oil in a saucepan and add 1 chopped onion, 1 chopped garlic clove, 3 deseeded and sliced red chillies, 1 tablespoon ground coriander, 2 teaspoons ground cumin and 1 cinnamon stick. Gently fry for 2–3 minutes until the onion has softened. Increase the heat to high, add 500 g (1 lb) minced lamb and fry, stirring, for 1–2 minutes until browned. Add 450 g (14½ oz) basmati rice and stir to coat, then stir in 800 ml (1 pint 8 fl oz) hot vegetable stock and 1 cored, deseeded and diced red pepper and bring to the boil. Cover tightly, reduce the heat to low and cook, undisturbed, for 15–20 minutes or until the liquid is absorbed and the rice is tender. Remove from the heat and stir in 4 tablespoons each of chopped coriander and mint leaves. Season and serve with dollops of yogurt.

Spicy Eggs with Merguez Sausages and Tomato

Serves 4

2 tablespoons olive oil

1 onion, finely sliced

1 red chilli, deseeded and finely chopped

1 garlic clove, crushed

300 g (10 oz) merguez sausages, roughly chopped

1 teaspoon dried oregano

400 g (13 oz) can cherry tomatoes

100 ml (3½ fl oz) passata with herbs

200 g (7 oz) roasted mixed peppers from a jar, drained and roughly chopped

4 eggs

salt and pepper

4 tablespoons finely chopped coriander leaves, to garnish

- Heat the oil in a large frying pan, add the onion, red chilli, garlic, merguez sausages and oregano and fry gently for about 5 minutes or until the onion is softened. Add the tomatoes, passata and peppers and cook for a further 5 minutes. If the sauce looks dry, add a splash of water.

- Season well, then make 4 hollows in the mixture, break an egg into each and cover the pan. Cook for 5 minutes or until the eggs are set.

- Divide between 4 warm serving plates, scatter with chopped coriander and serve immediately.

 Spicy Scrambled Eggs with Merguez Sausages Heat 2 tablespoons butter in a large frying pan until foaming, add 200 g (7 oz) thinly sliced merguez sausages and cook over a high heat for 3–4 minutes. Meanwhile, whisk together 6 eggs, 1 teaspoon garlic salt, 1 deseeded and chopped red chilli and 1 teaspoon dried oregano in a bowl, then add to the pan. Scramble together with the sausages and cook until the eggs are cooked to your liking. Serve with warm tortillas.

 Merguez Sausage and Tomato Tortilla Heat 2 tablespoons sunflower oil in a medium ovenproof frying pan, add 1 chopped onion, 200 g (7 oz) roughly chopped merguez sausages, 1 deseeded and chopped red chilli and 1 chopped garlic clove and cook over a medium heat for 3–4 minutes. Add 2 chopped tomatoes and cook for a further 3–4 minutes. Lightly beat 6 eggs in a bowl, then season and pour into the pan. Cook over a medium heat for 10–12 minutes or until the base is set, then place the pan under a preheated medium-hot grill and cook for 4–5 minutes or until the top is golden and set. Cut the tortilla into wedges and serve.

10 Spicy Beef Enchilada Wraps

Serves 4

8 corn tortillas

8 tablespoons hot chilli sauce

8 tablespoons shop-bought guacamole, plus extra to serve

8 tablespoons soured cream, plus extra to serve

¼ iceberg lettuce, shredded

400 g (13 oz) shop-bought ready-cooked roast beef slices, thickly sliced

8 tablespoons sliced green jalapeño chillies from a jar, drained

8 tablespoons shop-bought fresh salsa

salt and pepper

- Place 1 tortilla on a preheated hot griddle or in a dry frying pan and cook according to the packet instructions until heated through. Remove and keep warm, then repeat with the remaining tortillas.

- Lay the tortillas on a clean work surface and spread each one with 1 tablespoon each of the hot chilli sauce, guacamole and soured cream. Divide the lettuce between the tortillas, then top with the roast beef and 1 tablespoon each of the jalapeños and salsa. Season well.

- Roll up the filled tortillas to form wraps and serve immediately with extra guacamole and soured cream.

20 Spicy Enchilada Beef Rice

Heat 2 tablespoons sunflower oil in a large frying pan, add 1 chopped onion and 400 g (13 oz) minced beef and fry, stirring, over a high heat for 6–8 minutes until browned. Stir in a 375 g (12 oz) jar enchilada sauce and cook for 2–3 minutes or until bubbling. Add 500 g (1 lb) shop-bought ready-cooked long-grain rice and continue to stir and cook for 3–4 minutes or until piping hot. Season and serve immediately.

30 Spicy Beef Enchiladas

Heat 2 tablespoons sunflower oil in a large frying pan, add 1 chopped onion and 400 g (13 oz) minced beef and fry, stirring, over a high heat for 4–5 minutes or until browned. Spread half of a 395 g (13 oz) jar enchilada sauce over the base of a shallow, medium-sized baking dish. Divide the meat mixture between 8 corn tortillas and scatter over 300 g (10 oz) drained, sliced green jalapeño peppers from a jar. Roll up tightly and place in a single layer in the prepared dish, seam-side down. Spoon over the remaining enchilada sauce and sprinkle over 400 g (13 oz) grated Cheddar cheese. Cook under a preheated medium grill for 8–10 minutes or until the cheese is bubbling and golden. Serve with a green salad.

Chorizo, Spinach and Egg Salad with Paprika Croutons

Serves 4

1 tablespoon sunflower oil
4 eggs
200 g (7 oz) cooking chorizo, thickly sliced
4 handfuls of baby spinach leaves
salt and pepper

For the dressing

4 tablespoons extra-virgin olive oil
2 tablespoons red wine vinegar
2 teaspoons wholegrain mustard

For the croutons

½ ciabatta loaf, cut into bite-sized pieces
2 tablespoons olive oil
1 tablespoon smoked paprika

- To make the dressing, whisk together all the ingredients in a small bowl and set aside.

- To make the croutons, put the ciabatta in a bowl, toss in the olive oil and sprinkle with the paprika, then transfer to a baking sheet. Place in a preheated oven, 200°C (400°F), Gas Mark 6, for 10 minutes or until golden.

- Meanwhile, heat the sunflower oil in a large frying pan, add the eggs and fry to your liking, then remove and keep warm. Put the chorizo in a separate frying pan and dry-fry over a medium heat for 3–4 minutes or until crisp and cooked through.

- Put the chorizo and spinach in a large bowl, drizzle over a little of the dressing and toss to mix well. Divide between 4 serving plates, then top each with one-quarter of the croutons and an egg. Drizzle with the remaining dressing. Season to taste and serve immediately.

 Spicy Chorizo and Spinach Egg-Fried Rice Put 200 g (7 oz) spinach leaves in a saucepan, pour over boiling water to cover and leave to stand for 2 minutes or until wilted, then drain well and chop. Meanwhile, heat 2 tablespoons sunflower oil in a large wok or frying pan until hot, add 400 g (13 oz) diced chorizo and stir-fry for 2–3 minutes over a high heat. Add 500 g (1 lb) tub fresh egg-fried rice and the spinach and stir-fry for a further 2–3 minutes or until piping hot, then season. Serve immediately.

Spicy Chorizo and Spinach Frittata Put 200 g (7 oz) spinach leaves in a saucepan, pour over boiling water to cover and leave to stand for 2 minutes or until wilted, then drain well and chop. Meanwhile, heat 2 tablespoons sunflower oil in a medium ovenproof frying pan, add 2 finely chopped onions and cook over a medium-low heat for 8–10 minutes, stirring occasionally, until lightly browned and softened. Add 2 deseeded and chopped red chillies and 200 g (7 oz) roughly chopped chorizo and cook for a further 3–4 minutes, then add the spinach and stir to mix well. Lightly beat 6 eggs, then season and pour into the pan. Cook over a medium heat for 10–12 minutes or until the base is set, then place the pan under a preheated hot grill and cook for 4 minutes or until the top is golden and just set. Serve cut into wedges with a salad.

30 Spicy Ham and Pea Risotto

Serves 4

1 tablespoon olive oil

2 tablespoons butter

1 onion, chopped

1 teaspoon dried red chilli flakes

1 red chilli, deseeded and finely
  chopped

2 garlic cloves, crushed

250 g (8 oz) risotto rice, such
  as vialone nano, carnaroli
  or arborio

900 ml (1½ pints) hot chicken
  stock

200 g (7 oz) frozen peas

100 g (3½ oz) Parmesan cheese,
  grated

300 g (10 oz) cooked ham, diced

1 bunch of flat leaf parsley, finely
  chopped

salt and pepper

- Heat the oil and butter in a heavy-based saucepan, add the onion, chilli flakes, red chilli and garlic and cook over a medium heat for 3–4 minutes until softened and beginning to brown.

- Add the rice and stir for 1 minute or until the grains are well coated, then pour in 500 ml (17 fl oz) of the stock and cook until it has been absorbed, stirring frequently, then add the remaining stock and the peas and continue to cook, stirring continuously, until the liquid has been absorbed and the rice is tender but still firm (al dente).

- Stir in the Parmesan, ham and parsley, season to taste and serve immediately.

10 Spicy Ham and Pea Noodles

Heat 2 tablespoons sunflower oil in a wok or frying pan until hot, add 400 g (13 oz) cooked ham, cut into strips, 400 g (13 oz) frozen peas and a 120 g (4 oz) sachet spicy Szechuan tomato stir-fry sauce and stir-fry over a high heat for 2–3 minutes. Stir in a 400 g (13 oz) bag fresh egg noodles and stir-fry for 3–4 minutes or until piping hot. Serve immediately.

20 Spicy Ham and Pea Tortilla

Heat 2 tablespoons sunflower oil in a medium ovenproof frying pan, add 1 chopped onion, 2 deseeded and finely chopped red chillies, 3 chopped garlic cloves and 1 teaspoon smoked paprika and cook over a high heat for 2–3 minutes until softened, then add 400 g (13 oz) cooked ham, diced, and 300 g (10 oz) frozen peas and cook for a further 1–2 minutes. Lightly beat 6 eggs in a bowl, then season well and pour into the pan. Cook over a medium heat for 8–10 minutes or until the base is set, then place the pan under a preheated medium-hot grill and cook for 4–5 minutes or until the top is golden and set. Serve with a crisp green salad.

Spicy Sausage and Tomato Pasta

Serves 4

2 tablespoons olive oil

8 thick, spicy Italian sausages, cut into 2 cm (¾ inch) pieces

1 red chilli, deseeded and finely chopped

4 garlic cloves, finely chopped

1 onion, finely chopped

1 teaspoon dried red chilli flakes

400 g (13 oz) can chopped tomatoes with herbs

1 teaspoon caster sugar

2 teaspoons chopped rosemary

500 g (1 lb) fresh penne

salt and pepper

4 tablespoons chopped flat leaf parsley, to garnish

100 g (3½ oz) grated Parmesan cheese, to serve

- Heat the oil in a large frying pan, add the sausages and fry over a high heat for 3–4 minutes until browned. Add the red chilli, garlic, onion and chilli flakes and fry for a further 1–2 minutes.

- Stir in the tomatoes, sugar and rosemary and bring to the boil, then reduce the heat to medium and cook for 8–10 minutes.

- Meanwhile, cook the pasta in a large saucepan of salted boiling water according to the packet instructions until al dente. Drain well, then add to the sausage mixture. Season and toss to mix well.

- Spoon into warm bowls, scatter with chopped parsley and serve with the grated Parmesan.

 Spicy Sausage and Tomato Salad

Put a 400 g (13 oz) pack ready-cooked cocktail sausages, a 100 g (3½ oz) bag mixed salad leaves and 200 g (7 oz) halved cherry tomatoes in a salad bowl. Mix together 100 ml (3½ fl oz) shop-bought fresh Caesar salad dressing and 1 tablespoon chilli sauce in a small bowl. Pour the dressing over the salad, season and toss to mix well. Serve with crusty bread rolls.

 Spicy Sausage and Tomato Bake

Heat 2 tablespoons sunflower oil in a large frying pan, add 8 thick, spicy Italian sausages and fry over a high heat for 2–3 minutes or until lightly browned. Add 1 chopped onion, 3 chopped garlic cloves, 2 deseeded and chopped red chillies and fry for a further 2–3 minutes. Transfer to a shallow ovenproof dish, add a 400 g (13 oz) can chopped tomatoes, 1 teaspoon caster sugar and 1 teaspoon dried red chilli flakes, then season and toss to mix well. Place in a preheated oven, 200°C (400°F), Gas Mark 6, for 20–25 minutes or until the sausages are cooked through. Scatter over a small handful of chopped flat leaf parsley and serve with crusty bread.

30 Spicy Lamb and Vegetable Stew

Serves 4

1 tablespoon sunflower oil
600 g (1 lb 5 oz) lamb neck fillet, cut into 2 cm (¾ inch) cubes
1 onion, chopped
1 garlic clove, crushed
1 teaspoon peeled and grated fresh root ginger
2 tablespoons medium curry paste
1 large potato, peeled and cut into 2 cm (¾ inch) cubes
1 large carrot, peeled and cut into 2 cm (¾ inch) cubes
400 ml (14 fl oz) hot lamb stock
200 ml (7 fl oz) canned coconut milk
200 g (7 oz) frozen peas
small handful of coriander leaves, to garnish
steamed rice, to serve (optional)

- Heat the oil in a large heavy-based saucepan, add the lamb, onion, garlic and ginger and cook over a high heat for 3–4 minutes, stirring frequently, until the lamb is browned and the onion is softened. Reduce the heat to medium, add the curry paste and cook, stirring, for a further 1–2 minutes.

- Stir in the potato, carrot, stock and coconut milk and bring to the boil. Cook, uncovered, for 15–20 minutes or until the lamb and vegetables are tender. Stir in the peas 3 minutes before the end of the cooking time.

- Ladle into warm bowls, scatter with the coriander leaves and serve with steamed rice, if liked.

---

1 Grilled Spicy Lamb Cutlets

Mix together 2 tablespoons medium or hot curry paste and 6 tablespoons natural yogurt in a bowl, then spread the mixture all over 12 lamb cutlets and season. Cook under a preheated hot grill for 2–3 minutes on each side or until cooked to your liking. Serve with warm flatbreads and a salad.

2 Spicy Lamb and Vegetable Curry

Heat 2 tablespoons sunflower oil in a large wok or frying pan until hot, add 1 chopped onion, 2 chopped garlic cloves and 1 teaspoon peeled and grated fresh root ginger and stir-fry over a high heat for 1–2 minutes, then add 600 g (1 lb 5 oz) minced lamb, 3 tablespoons medium curry paste, 200 g (7 oz) peeled potatoes, cut into 1 cm (½ inch) cubes, and 200 g (7 oz) peeled carrots, cut into 1 cm (½ inch) cubes, and stir-fry for a further 1–2 minutes until the lamb is browned. Pour in 200 ml (7 fl oz) canned coconut milk and cook, uncovered, over a medium heat for 10–12 minutes, stirring frequently, until the lamb and vegetables are tender. Season, then serve immediately with steamed rice or crusty bread.

30 Sticky Spicy Pork with Vegetable Noodles

Serves 4

1 kg (2¼ lb) thick streaky
   pork rashers
2 tablespoons chilli sauce
6 tablespoons hoisin sauce
2 tablespoons oyster sauce
200 ml (7 fl oz) water
200 g (7 oz) mangetout
2 carrots, peeled and cut into
   matchsticks
2 red chillies, deseeded and
   finely chopped
2 teaspoons peeled and grated
   fresh root ginger
2 tablespoons toasted sesame oil
300 g (10 oz) pack ready-cooked
   medium egg noodles
25 g (1 oz) mint leaves, chopped

- Bring a large saucepan of water to the boil, add the pork rashers, bring back to the boil and cook for 1 minute. Drain, pat dry with kitchen paper and put on a baking sheet.

- Mix together the chilli sauce, 4 tablespoons of the hoisin sauce and the oyster sauce in a bowl, pour over the pork and toss to mix well. Place in a preheated oven, 240°C (475°F), Gas Mark 9, for 20 minutes or until sticky and cooked through.

- Meanwhile, bring the measurement water to the boil in a large wok or frying pan, add the mangetout, carrots, red chillies and ginger, cover and cook for 2 minutes. Add the oil, noodles and remaining hoisin sauce and heat through for 2 minutes, then add the mint and toss to mix well.

- Divide the noodles between warm bowls and serve immediately topped with the pork rashers.

 **Grilled Spicy Pork** Mix together 2 tablespoons chilli sauce, 2 tablespoons sweet chilli sauce and 1 tablespoon hoisin sauce in a bowl, then spread the mixture all over 4 thin pork escalopes. Cook under a preheated hot grill for 3–4 minutes on each side or until cooked through. Serve with steamed rice or noodles.

2 Spicy Pork, Vegetable and Noodle Stir-Fry Cook 2 pork chops, about 200 g (7 oz) each, under a preheated hot grill for 5–6 minutes on each side or until cooked through. Cool slightly, then finely dice and set aside. Heat 2 tablespoons sunflower oil in a large wok or frying pan until hot, add 8 finely sliced spring onions, 4 chopped garlic cloves, 1 teaspoon peeled and grated fresh root ginger, 1 deseeded and finely chopped red chilli and stir-fry over a high heat for 1 minute. Add a 300 g (10 oz) pack ready-prepared stir-fry vegetable noodles, a 300 g (10 oz) bag fresh egg noodles, a 120 g (4 oz) sachet hoisin stir-fry sauce and 1 tablespoon chilli sauce and stir-fry for a further 3–4 minutes. Add the diced pork and continue to stir-fry for 2–3 minutes until piping hot, tossing to mix well. Serve immediately.

Veal and Spring Onion Skewers with Sweet Chilli Dip

Serves 4

400 g (13 oz) veal fillet, cut into bite-sized pieces

8–10 spring onions, cut into 2 cm (¾ inch) lengths

2 red peppers, cored, deseeded and cut into bite-sized pieces

8 tablespoons sweet chilli sauce

1 tablespoon hot chilli sauce

finely grated rind and juice of 2 limes

4 tablespoons kecap manis (thick soy sauce)

- Thread the veal pieces on to 12 metal skewers, alternating with pieces of spring onion and red pepper.

- Whisk together the remaining ingredients a small bowl, then transfer half to a serving dish and set aside. Brush the remaining mixture over the skewers on both sides until evenly coated. Cover and leave to marinate for 10 minutes.

- Cook the skewers on a preheated barbecue or under a preheated medium-hot grill for 4–5 minutes on each side or until the meat is cooked through.

- Transfer the skewers on to 4 serving plates and serve with the reserved marinade for dipping.

Sweet Chilli Veal and Spring Onion Rice

Heat 2 tablespoons sunflower oil in a large wok or frying pan until hot, add 500 g (1 lb) minced veal and 6 sliced spring onions and stir-fry over a high heat for 1–2 minutes until lightly browned. Add 500 g (1 lb) shop-bought ready-cooked rice, 4 tablespoons sweet chilli sauce, 1 teaspoon hot chilli sauce and 2 teaspoons light soy sauce and stir-fry for a further 3–4 minutes or until piping hot and cooked through. Serve immediately.

Sweet Chilli Veal and Spring Onion

Noodles Heat 2 tablespoons sunflower oil in a heavy-based saucepan until hot, add 500 g (1 lb) minced veal and cook over a high heat for 2–3 minutes until lightly browned. Add 8 sliced spring onions, 1 deseeded and finely chopped red chilli, 1 teaspoon ginger paste, 1 teaspoon garlic paste and 6 tablespoons sweet chilli sauce and cook for a further 3–4 minutes. Add 600 ml (1 pint) hot vegetable stock and 500 g (1 lb) pack ready-cooked medium egg noodles and place in a preheated oven, 200°C (400°F), Gas Mark 6, for 15 minutes or until piping hot and the noodles are cooked through and the veal is tender. Season, toss to mix well and serve immediately.

Thai Pork Larb Salad

Serves 4

2 tablespoons vegetable oil

6 spring onions, thinly sliced

2 garlic cloves, finely chopped

2 teaspoons peeled and grated
  fresh root ginger

1 red chilli, deseeded and
  finely chopped

2 cm (¾ inch) length of trimmed
  lemon grass stalk, finely chopped

350 g (11½ oz) minced pork

3 tablespoons fish sauce

2 tablespoons Chinese rice wine

4 tablespoons sweet chilli sauce

juice of 1 lime

2 tablespoons runny honey

100 g (3½ oz) glass noodles

small handful of coriander, chopped

small handful of mint, chopped

8–12 large iceberg lettuce leaves

100 g (3½ oz) chopped chilli-
  roasted peanuts, to serve

- Heat the oil in a large wok or frying pan until hot, add the spring onions, garlic, ginger, red chilli and lemon grass and stir-fry over a high heat for 30 seconds, then add the pork and stir-fry for a further 4–5 minutes or until browned and cooked through.

- Stir in the fish sauce, rice wine, chilli sauce, lime juice and honey, reduce the heat and simmer for 2 minutes, then remove the pan from the heat.

- Meanwhile, put the noodles in a heatproof bowl and cover with boiling water. Soak for 3–4 minutes, then drain and cut into short strands with kitchen scissors.

- Add the noodles to the pork mixture and mix through. Return the pan to the heat and cook over a high heat for 3–4 minutes or until piping hot. Remove from the heat and stir in the chopped herbs.

- Spoon the mixture into the lettuce leaves and transfer to 4 serving plates. Serve sprinkled with the chopped peanuts.

Spicy Thai Scrambled Eggs

with Pork Heat 2 tablespoons sunflower oil in a frying pan. Add 200g minced pork and 1 tablespoon thai red curry paste and stir fry over a high heat for 1–2 minutes. Stir in 6 beaten eggs and continue to cook over a high heat, stirring, for 2–3 minutes. Remove from the heat and serve on toasted bread.

Thai Green Pork Rice

Heat 2 tablespoons sunflower oil in a heavy-based saucepan, add 6 sliced spring onions, 2 chopped garlic cloves, 1 teaspoon grated fresh root ginger, 1 deseeded and chopped red chilli, a 2 cm (¾ inch) length of trimmed lemon grass stalk, finely chopped, 400 g (13 oz) minced pork and 1 tablespoon green curry paste and fry, stirring, over a high heat for 1–2 minutes until the pork is browned. Add 450 g (14 ½ oz) jasmine rice and stir until well coated, then pour in 600 ml (1 pint) hot vegetable stock and 200 ml (7 fl oz) canned coconut milk and bring to the boil. Cover tightly, reduce the heat to low and cook, undisturbed, for 15–20 minutes or until the liquid is absorbed and the rice is tender. Remove from the heat and leave to stand for a few minutes before serving.

30 West Indian Curried Beef and Black Bean Stew

Serves 4

3 tablespoons sunflower oil
800 g (1¾ lb) minced beef
6 whole cloves
1 onion, finely chopped
2 tablespoons medium curry
  powder
2 carrots, peeled and cut into 1 cm
  (½ inch) cubes
2 celery sticks, diced
1 tablespoon thyme leaves
2 garlic cloves, crushed
4 tablespoons tomato purée
600 ml (1 pint) hot beef stock
1 large potato, peeled and cut into
  1 cm (½ inch) cubes
200 g (7 oz) canned black beans,
  rinsed and drained
200 g (7 oz) canned black-eyed
  beans, rinsed and drained
salt and pepper
lemon wedges, to serve

- Heat the oil in a large heavy-based saucepan, add the beef and fry, stirring. over a medium-high heat for 5–6 minutes or until browned.

- Add the cloves, onion and curry powder and cook for 2–3 minutes until the onions are beginning to soften, then stir in the carrots, celery, thyme, garlic and tomato purée.

- Pour in the beef stock to just cover the meat and stir well, then add the potato and beans and bring to the boil. Reduce the heat slightly and simmer for 20 minutes, uncovered, or until the potatoes and beef are tender, then season to taste.

- Ladle into warm bowls and serve with lemon wedges.

10 Curried Beef and Black Bean Stir-Fry

Heat 2 tablespoons sunflower oil in a large wok until hot, add 500 g (1 lb) minced beef and 1 tablespoon medium curry paste and stir-fry over a high heat for 3–4 minutes until browned. Add 100 ml (3½ fl oz) canned coconut milk and 200 g (7 oz) rinsed and drained canned black beans and stir-fry for a further 3–4 minutes or until piping hot and cooked through. Season and serve immediately with noodles.

20 Curried Beef and Black Bean Pilau

Heat 2 tablespoons sunflower oil in a large wok or frying pan until hot, add 500 g (1 lb) minced beef and 1 tablespoon medium curry paste and stir-fry over a high heat for 2–3 minutes until browned. Add 100 ml (3½ fl oz) canned coconut milk, reduce the heat to medium and simmer gently for 6–8 minutes or until most of the liquid has been absorbed and the beef is cooked through. Stir in 500 g (1 lb) shop-bought ready-cooked long-grain or basmati rice and 200 g (7 oz) rinsed and drained canned black beans and heat through for 2–3 minutes or until piping hot. Season, then serve immediately.

Five-Spice Pork Chops with Green Beans

Serves 4

2 garlic cloves, very finely
  chopped

2 red chillies, deseeded and
  finely chopped

2 teaspoons five-spice powder

4 tablespoons sweet chilli sauce

2 tablespoons dark soy sauce

4 pork chops, about 200 g
  (7 oz) each

300 g (10 oz) green beans,
  trimmed

2 tablespoons extra-virgin
  olive oil

1 tablespoon finely grated
  lemon rind

juice of ½ lemon

salt and pepper

- Mix together the garlic, red chillies, five-spice powder, sweet chilli sauce and soy sauce in a small bowl, then spread the mixture all over the pork chops and season. Cover and leave to marinate for 10 minutes.

- Put the pork chops on a baking sheet lined with foil, then cook under a preheated hot grill for 5–6 minutes on each side or until cooked through.

- Meanwhile, cook the beans in a large saucepan of lightly salted boiling water for 3–4 minutes until just tender. Drain well, then put in a bowl with the olive oil, lemon rind and juice and toss together. Cover and keep warm.

- Transfer the pork chops on to warm serving plates and serve with the green beans.

 Spicy Pork and Vegetable Stir-Fry

Heat 2 tablespoons sunflower oil in a large wok or frying pan until hot, add 400 g (13 oz) pork tenderloin fillet, cut into thin strips, and stir-fry over a high heat for 2–3 minutes until browned. Add a 300 g pack ready-prepared stir-fry vegetables and a 120 g (4 oz) sachet sweet chilli stir-fry sauce and stir-fry for a further 3–4 minutes or until piping hot and the pork is cooked through. Serve immediately with rice or noodles.

Spicy Pork and Vegetable Broth

Heat 2 tablespoons sunflower oil in a large heavy-based saucepan, add 1 chopped onion, 2 deseeded and chopped red chillies, 2 teaspoons peeled and grated fresh root ginger, 2 teaspoons grated garlic and 1 teaspoon five-spice powder and cook over a medium heat for 3–4 minutes, stirring occasionally, until the onion is softened. Add 500 g (1 lb) pork tenderloin fillet, cubed, and 100 g (3½ oz) long-grain rice and cook, stirring, for 2–3 minutes until the pork browned. Pour in 1 litre (1¾ pints) hot chicken stock and bring to the boil, then reduce the heat to medium and cook, uncovered, for 20 minutes until the pork is cooked through and the rice is tender, adding 400 g (13 oz) mixed frozen vegetables 4–5 minutes before the end of the cooking time. Season, then serve immediately.

QuickCook
Fish and Seafood

Recipes listed by cooking time

30 Spicy Herb and Coconut Salmon Parcels

Serves 4

fresh banana leaves (optional)
4 thick skinless salmon fillets,
   about 200 g (7 oz) each
juice of 1 lime, for drizzling

For the spice paste

2 teaspoons ground cumin
2 teaspoons ground coriander
1½ teaspoons golden caster sugar
150 g (5 oz) grated fresh coconut
2 red chillies, deseeded and finely
   chopped, plus extra to garnish
50 g (2 oz) chopped coriander leaves
4 tablespoons chopped mint leaves
3 garlic cloves, crushed
1 teaspoon grated fresh root ginger
juice of 1 lime
3 tablespoons vegetable oil
salt

To serve

lime wedges
pilau rice

- Cut the banana leaves, if using, into four 24 cm (9½ inch) squares, then soften by dipping into a saucepan of very hot water for a few seconds. As they become pliant, remove the leaves from the pan and pat dry with kitchen paper.

- To make the spice paste, put all the ingredients in a mini food processor and blend to a paste, then season with salt.

- Place the banana leaf squares on a clean work surface. Spread the paste liberally on both sides of each piece of fish, then drizzle with the lime juice. Place a piece of fish on a banana leaf and wrap up like a parcel, securing with bamboo skewers or kitchen string. Repeat with the remaining fish to make 4 parcels. Alternatively, place the fish on 4 large squares of foil and seal well to form parcels.

- Place the parcels on a baking sheet and bake in a preheated oven, 200°C (400°F), Gas Mark 6, for 15–20 minutes or until cooked through.

- Transfer the parcels on to serving plates, unwrap and sprinkle with extra chopped chilli. Serve with lime wedges to squeeze over and pilau rice.

---

10 Spicy Salmon and Herb Salad

Arrange 2 x 120 g (4 oz) bags herb salad in a large serving dish. Flake 500 g (1 lb) hot-smoked salmon fillets into the salad, removing any bones. Mix together the juice of 2 limes, 1 deseeded and chopped red chilli, 1 teaspoon honey, 1 teaspoon ground cumin and 6 tablespoons olive oil in a bowl, then season. Drizzle over the salad, toss to mix well and serve.

20 Spicy Salmon and Herb Rice

Heat 2 tablespoons sunflower oil in a large wok or frying pan until hot, add 4 sliced shallots and cook over a medium-low heat, stirring occasionally, for 10–12 minutes or until softened and lightly golden. Increase the heat to high, add 2 teaspoons cumin seeds, 1 tablespoon mild curry powder, 1 deseeded and chopped red chilli and 500 g (1 lb) skinless salmon fillets, boned and cut into bite-sized pieces, and stir-fry for 2–3 minutes or until the fish is almost cooked through. Add 500 g (1 lb) shop-bought ready-cooked basmati rice and stir-fry for a further 2–3 minutes or until piping hot, then season. Remove from the heat and stir in a small handful each of chopped mint and coriander leaves. Serve immediately.

 Chilli Spaghetti Vongole

Serves 4

450 g (14½ oz) dried spaghetti
6 tablespoons extra-virgin olive oil, plus extra to serve
2 garlic cloves, chopped
2 red chillies, deseeded and finely chopped
4 anchovy fillets in oil, drained and chopped
small handful of flat leaf parsley, finely chopped
1 kg (2¼ lb) fresh clams, scrubbed
100 ml (3½ fl oz) dry white wine
salt and pepper

- Cook the pasta in a large saucepan of salted boiling water according to the packet instructions until al dente. Drain, then return to the pan

- Meanwhile, heat the oil in a frying pan, add the garlic, red chillies, anchovies and half the parsley and fry gently for a couple of minutes. Add the clams to the pan, discarding any that are cracked or don't shut when tapped. Pour in the wine, then increase the heat to high, cover tightly and cook for 4–5 minutes or until the clams have opened. Discard any that remain closed.

- Add the clams and the juices to the spaghetti with the remaining parsley, then season and toss to mix well. Divide into warm bowls, drizzle with a little extra olive oil and serve immediately.

 Clam and Chilli Rice

Heat 2 tablespoons sunflower oil in a wok or frying pan until hot, add 2 deseeded and finely diced red chillies, 1 teaspoon garlic paste, 2 rinsed and drained 280 g (9 oz) cans clams in brine and 500 g (1 lb) shop-bought ready-cooked long-grain rice and stir-fry over a high heat for 3–4 minutes or until piping hot, then season. Remove from the heat and stir in a small handful of chopped flat leaf parsley. Serve immediately.

 Chilli and Garlic– Braised Clams

Heat 2 tablespoons olive oil in a heavy-based saucepan, add 4 chopped shallots and cook over a medium heat, stirring occasionally, for 6–8 minutes until softened. Add 2 crushed garlic cloves, 2 deseeded and finely chopped red chillies and cook, stirring, for 1–2 minutes. Stir in 2 tablespoons tomato purée and 4 finely chopped plum tomatoes and cook for a further 8–10 minutes. Add 500 ml (17 fl oz) hot fish stock and 800 g

(1¾ lb) fresh scrubbed clams, discarding any that are cracked or don't shut when tapped, then bring to the boil, cover tightly and cook for 4–5 minutes or until the clams have opened. Discard any that remain closed. Season, ladle into warm bowls and serve.

Creamy Curried Mussel Soup

Serves 4

1 tablespoon butter

2 shallots, thinly sliced

2 garlic cloves, crushed

1 teaspoon peeled and finely
  grated fresh root ginger

2 large red chillies, deseeded and
  finely diced

1 teaspoon medium curry powder

1 large pinch of saffron threads

100 ml (3½ fl oz) dry white wine

400 ml (14 fl oz) hot vegetable
  stock

1 kg (2¼ lb) fresh mussels,
  scrubbed and debearded

200 ml (7 fl oz) double cream

6 tablespoons finely chopped
  coriander leaves

salt and pepper

• Heat the butter in a large wok or frying pan, add the shallots, garlic, ginger, red chillies and curry powder and stir-fry over a high heat for 1 minute. Add the saffron, white wine and stock and bring to the boil, then reduce the heat to medium and cook for 1–2 minutes.

• Add the mussels to the pan, discarding any that are cracked or don't shut when tapped. Increase the heat to high, cover tightly and cook for 2–3 minutes, shaking the pan occasionally, until the mussels have opened. Discard any that remain closed. Remove the mussels with a slotted spoon and set aside.

• Add the cream to the stock mixture and bring back to the boil, then reduce the heat and simmer gently, uncovered, for 5–6 minutes. Return the mussels to the pan, stir in the coriander and season to taste.

• Ladle into warm soup bowls and serve with crusty bread.

 ### Curried Smoked Mussel Omelette

Whisk together 4 eggs and 2 teaspoons hot curry powder in a bowl, then season with salt. Heat 2 tablespoons butter in a large frying pan and add the egg mixture, swirling to coat evenly. Cook for 1–2 minutes and then add a drained 85 g (3 oz) can smoked mussels in olive oil down the centre. Fold the egg mixture over the mussels. Flip to seal and cook for 1–2 minutes. Keep warm while you repeat the recipe, to make 2 omelettes in total. Divide each omelette in two and serve one half per person.

 ### Creamy Curried Mussel Pilau

Heat 1 tablespoon butter and 1 tablespoon sunflower oil in a heavy-based saucepan, add 4 sliced shallots and cook, stirring, for 2–3 minutes until softened. Add a large pinch of saffron threads, 1 tablespoon medium curry powder and 450 g (14½ oz) basmati rice and stir for 1–2 minutes until the rice is well coated, then add 2 x 175 g (6 oz) packs ready-cooked and shelled mussels. Pour in 650 ml (1 pint 2 fl oz) hot fish stock and 150 ml (¼ pint) double cream, season and bring to the boil. Cover tightly, reduce the heat to low and cook, undisturbed, for 15–20 minutes or until the liquid is absorbed and the rice is tender. Remove from the heat and leave to stand for a few minutes before serving.

Chilli and Coriander Crab Cakes

Serves 4

400 g (13 oz) fresh white crabmeat
200 g (7 oz) raw peeled tiger
  prawns, roughly chopped
1 tablespoon hot curry paste
2 garlic cloves, minced
1 red chilli, deseeded and
  finely chopped
1 red onion, finely chopped
4 tablespoons chopped coriander
  leaves, plus extra to garnish
1 small egg, beaten
100 g (3½ oz) fresh white
  breadcrumbs
sunflower oil, for brushing
salt and pepper

To serve

lemon wedges
green salad

- Put the crabmeat, prawns, curry paste, garlic, red chilli, red onion, coriander, egg and breadcrumbs in a food processor or blender. Season well, then blend for a few seconds until well mixed. Transfer to a bowl then, using your fingers, combine further to make a thick patty-like mixture.

- Line a baking sheet with nonstick baking parchment and brush with a little oil. Using wet hands, divide the crab mixture into 12 equal portions and shape each one into a round cake. Transfer the crab cakes on to the prepared baking sheet, brush with a little oil and bake in a preheated oven, 200°C (400°F), Gas Mark 6, for 15–20 minutes or until lightly browned and cooked through.

- Transfer on to 4 serving plates and serve with lemon wedges to squeeze over and a crisp green salad.

---

10 Warm Crab and Chilli Rice Salad

Heat a large nonstick wok or frying pan until hot, add 400 g (13 oz) shop-bought ready-cooked fresh rice and stir-fry over a high heat for 3–4 minutes or until piping hot. Remove from the heat and stir in 400 g (13 oz) cooked white crabmeat, a handful of chopped coriander and a small handful of chopped mint. Transfer to a large serving dish. Mix 1 deseeded and diced red chilli, 6 tablespoons olive oil and the juice of 2 limes, then season. Pour the dressing over the salad, toss to mix and serve.

20 Crab, Chilli and Coriander Pasta

Cook 375 g (12 oz) linguine in a large saucepan of salted boiling water according to the packet instructions until al dente. Meanwhile, heat 3 tablespoons olive oil in a large frying pan, add 4 finely chopped garlic cloves and 1 deseeded and finely chopped red chilli and fry over a medium-low heat, stirring occasionally, for 4–5 minutes until softened. Add 400 g (13 oz) fresh white crabmeat and cook for a further 2–3 minutes or until piping hot. Drain the pasta and add to the crab mixture with a large handful of chopped coriander leaves. Season, toss to mix well and serve immediately.

30 Haddock, Tomato and Tamarind Fish Curry

Serves 4

750 g (1 lb 10 oz) skinless haddock
  fillets, boned and cut into chunks
1 tablespoon tamarind paste
4 tablespoons rice wine vinegar
2 tablespoons cumin seeds
1 teaspoon ground turmeric
2 teaspoons hot curry powder
1 teaspoon salt
4 tablespoons sunflower oil
1 onion, finely chopped
3 garlic cloves, finely grated
2 teaspoons grated fresh root ginger
2 teaspoons black mustard seeds or
  nigella seeds (black onion seeds)
600 g (1 lb 5 oz) canned chopped
  tomatoes
1 teaspoon caster sugar
200 g (7 oz) cherry tomatoes
chopped coriander, to garnish

To serve

poppadums
steamed basmati rice (optional)

- Put the fish in a shallow non-reactive bowl. Mix together the tamarind, vinegar, cumin seeds, turmeric, curry powder and salt in a small bowl. Spoon over the fish and toss to coat evenly, then cover and leave to marinate.

- Meanwhile, heat the oil in a large wok or frying pan over a high heat until hot, add the onion, garlic, ginger and mustard or nigella seeds, then reduce the heat to medium and stir-fry for 1–2 minutes.

- Add the chopped tomatoes and sugar, stir through and bring to the boil. Reduce the heat again, cover and cook gently, stirring occasionally, for 15–20 minutes.

- Add the cherry tomatoes and the fish with its marinade and stir gently to mix. Cover and simmer gently for 5–6 minutes or until the fish is cooked through and flakes easily.

- Ladle into warm bowls, scatter with chopped coriander and serve with poppadums and steamed basmati rice, if liked.

 Grilled Tomato and Tamarind Haddock

Mix together 1 teaspoon tamarind paste, 1 teaspoon tomato purée, 1 tablespoon hot curry powder and 2 tablespoons sunflower oil in a bowl, then spread the mixture over 4 skinless haddock fillets, about 150–160 g (5–5½ oz) each, and season with salt. Cook under a preheated hot grill for 6–8 minutes or until just cooked through. Serve with salad or steamed rice.

Baked Tamarind Haddock with Cherry Tomatoes Mix together 1 teaspoon tamarind paste, 1 tablespoon hot curry powder, 2 tablespoons sunflower oil, 2 crushed garlic cloves and 1 teaspoon peeled and grated fresh root ginger in a bowl, then spread the mixture over 4 skinless haddock fillets, about 150–160 g (5–5½ oz) each, and season with salt. Place in an ovenproof dish and scatter over 400 g (13 oz) cherry tomatoes. Place in a preheated oven, 220°C (425°F), Gas Mark 7, for 12–15 minutes or until the fish is cooked through. Serve with steamed rice and salad.

HOT-FISH-PAR

Lemon Sole with Spicy Salsa

Serves 4

4 lemon sole fillets, 225 g (7½ oz)
    each, skinned

salt and pepper

For the salsa

1 ripe mango, peeled, stoned and
    finely diced

1 red pepper, cored, deseeded and
    finely chopped

100 g (3½ oz) cherry tomatoes,
    quartered

1 red onion, finely chopped

½ teaspoon caster sugar

1 red chilli, deseeded and
    finely chopped

4 tablespoons chopped coriander
    leaves, plus extra to garnish

2 tablespoons rice vinegar

finely grated rind and juice of 1 lime

1 teaspoon chilli oil

2 tablespoons olive oil

To serve

lime wedges

steamed basmati rice

- To make the salsa, mix together all the ingredients in a large bowl and season well.

- Place the fish fillets on a clean work surface, skinned-side up, and cut into half lengthways. Spoon some of the salsa on to the tail ends of the fish, roll up tightly, then season and place in a large nonstick frying pan. Cover and cook over a low heat for 8–10 minutes. Remove the lid and cook, uncovered, for a further 3 minutes or until cooked through.

- Transfer the fish on to serving plates and scatter with chopped coriander. Serve with the remaining salsa, lime wedges to squeeze over and steamed basmati rice.

 Fish and Spicy Salsa Salad

Make the salsa in a large salad bowl as above and add the torn leaves of 1 Romaine lettuce. Flake 400 g (13 oz) hot-smoked salmon or trout fillets into large pieces, removing any bones, and add to the salad. Drizzle over 120 ml (4 fl oz) thousand island dressing, toss to mix well.

 Mexican Fish and Salsa Bake

Place 4 thick skinless white fish fillets, about 175 g (6 oz) each, in a single layer in a shallow ovenproof dish and season well. Finely dice 3 plum tomatoes, 1 small red onion, 2 deseeded red chillies, 2 garlic cloves and 100 g (3½ oz) mango flesh and mix together in a bowl. Stir in the finely grated rind and juice of 1 lime, 2 tablespoons sunflower oil and 1 teaspoon cumin seeds. Season, then spoon the mixture over the prepared fish fillets. Place in a preheated oven, 200°C (400°F), Gas Mark 6, for 20 minutes or until cooked through. Serve immediately.

30 Griddled Piri Piri Squid with Mint and Coriander

Serves 4

800 g (1¾ lb) squid, cleaned and
  tentacles removed
finely grated rind and juice of
  1 lime
1 teaspoon ground cumin
2 teaspoons piri piri seasoning
1 red chilli, deseeded and
  finely diced
1 teaspoon sea salt
1 garlic clove, crushed
4 tablespoons olive oil, plus extra
  to serve
½ cucumber
small handful of mint leaves,
  roughly chopped
small handful of coriander leaves,
  roughly chopped
lime wedges, to serve (optional)

- Cut down the side of the squid so that it can be laid flat on a chopping board. Using a sharp knife, lightly score the inside flesh in a crisscross pattern, which will help to tenderize it, and cut into bite-sized pieces.

- Put the squid pieces in a shallow non-reactive bowl. Mix together the lime rind, cumin, piri piri seasoning, red chilli, sea salt, garlic and oil in a small bowl, then rub into the squid. Cover and leave to marinate for 10–15 minutes.

- Meanwhile, using a mandolin, finely shred the cucumber and set aside.

- Heat a nonstick, ridged griddle pan until smoking hot. Remove the squid from the marinade, add to the griddle pan and cook for no more than 2 minutes on each side, pushing the squid down with the back of a fish slice, until it is just cooked through. Transfer to a large shallow bowl.

- Add the cucumber and chopped herbs to the bowl and toss to mix well. Serve immediately, with a drizzle of extra olive oil and lime wedges, if liked.

Piri Piri Squid and Seafood Salad

Put 2 x 240 g (8 oz) packs mixed ready-cooked seafood with squid and a 200 g (7 oz) bag mixed salad leaves in a salad bowl. Mix together 2 teaspoons piri piri seasoning and 150 ml (¼ pint) thousand island dressing in a small bowl, then season. Pour the dressing over the salad, toss to mix well and serve immediately.

Crispy Fried Piri Piri Squid

Fill a large saucepan one-quarter full with sunflower oil and heat to 180–190°C (350–370°F), or until a cube of bread browns in 30 seconds. Meanwhile, mix together 200 g (7 oz) gram flour, 2 tablespoons piri piri seasoning and 1 teaspoon sea salt in a large bowl. Add a little cold water to the flour mixture to make a thick batter

(resembling thick double cream). Cut 600 g (1 lb 5 oz) cleaned squid, tentacles discarded, into thick rings and dip into the batter. Remove the squid rings from the batter and deep-fry in batches for 1–2 minutes or until they turn golden and crispy. Remove with a slotted spoon and drain on kitchen paper. Serve immediately.

30 Prawn and Salmon Laksa

Serves 4

1 tablespoon sunflower oil
8 spring onions, thickly sliced,
   plus extra, shredded, to garnish
3 garlic cloves, finely chopped
1 red chilli, deseeded and finely
   chopped, plus extra to garnish
3 teaspoons grated fresh root ginger
2 tablespoons lemon grass paste
2 tablespoons laksa curry paste
400 ml (14 fl oz) can coconut milk
400 ml (14 fl oz) hot chicken stock
500 g (1 lb) skinless salmon fillets,
   boned and cut into cubes
12 cooked king prawns, peeled
   and deveined, with tails left on
small handful of fresh bean sprouts
2 tablespoons chopped coriander
   leaves, plus extra to garnish
1 teaspoon fish sauce
1 tablespoon light soy sauce
250 g (8 oz) dried rice noodles
¼ cucumber, cut into matchsticks
salt and pepper

- Heat the oil in a large wok or frying pan until hot, add the spring onions, garlic, red chilli, ginger, lemon grass paste and curry paste and stir-fry over a high heat for 2–3 minutes. Pour in the coconut milk and stock and bring to the boil, then simmer gently for 4–5 minutes.

- Add the salmon and bring to the boil, then reduce the heat to low and simmer, uncovered, for 5–7 minutes or until the fish is just cooked through. Add the prawns, bean sprouts, coriander, fish sauce and soy sauce and heat through for a few minutes until piping hot, then season to taste. Keep warm.

- Cook the noodles according to the packet instructions, then drain and divide into warm bowls. Top with the salmon and prawns, then ladle over the laksa broth. Scatter over the cucumber, extra spring onions, red chilli and coriander leaves and serve immediately.

 Hot Salmon and Prawn Laksa Rice

Heat 2 tablespoons sunflower oil in a large wok until hot, add 500 g (1 lb) shop-bought ready-cooked rice and 1 tablespoon laksa curry paste and stir-fry over a high heat for 3–4 minutes. Stir in 400 g (13 oz) flaked hot-smoked salmon fillets, bones removed, and 400 g (13 oz) cooked peeled prawns and toss to mix well. Heat through and serve.

 Laksa Salmon and Prawn Omelette

Heat 2 tablespoons sunflower oil in a medium ovenproof frying pan, add 6 finely sliced spring onions and 1 deseeded and chopped red chilli and cook, stirring, for 1–2 minutes. Meanwhile, whisk together 6 eggs, 1 tablespoon laksa curry paste and a small handful of finely chopped coriander leaves in a bowl. Add to the pan with 300 g (10 oz) flaked hot-smoked salmon fillets, bones removed, and 400 g (13 oz) cooked peeled tiger prawns. Cook over a medium heat for 10–12 minutes or until the base is set, then place the pan under a preheated medium-hot grill and cook for 3–4 minutes or until the top is lightly golden and just set. Serve immediately with a crisp salad.

HOT-FISH-VIT

Spicy Monkfish and Mixed Pepper Stew

Serves 4

2 tablespoons vegetable oil

2 onions, finely chopped

2 tablespoons medium or hot curry powder

1 teaspoon ground turmeric

900 g (2 lb) monkfish tail, cut into bite-sized pieces

2 garlic cloves, chopped

1 teaspoon peeled and finely grated fresh root ginger

½ teaspoon tamarind paste

1 tablespoon thyme leaves

1 star anise

450 ml (¾ pint) hot fish stock

1 red pepper, cored, deseeded and cut into 3 cm (1 inch) pieces

1 yellow pepper, cored, deseeded and cut into 3 cm (1 inch) pieces

steamed rice, to serve (optional)

- Heat the oil in a heavy-based saucepan, add the onions and cook over a medium heat, stirring occasionally, for 2–3 minutes until softened. Stir in the curry powder and turmeric and cook for a further 1 minute until fragrant.

- Add the remaining ingredients and stir together well. Bring to a simmer, then reduce the heat to low and cook, uncovered, for 8–10 minutes or until the fish is cooked through and the peppers are tender.

- Ladle into warm bowls and serve with steamed rice, if liked.

 Chinese Monkfish and Mixed Pepper Stir-Fry Core, deseed and finely slice 1 red pepper and 1 yellow pepper. Heat 2 tablespoons sunflower oil in a large wok or frying pan until hot, add the peppers and 600 g (1 lb 5 oz) monkfish tail, cubed, and stir-fry over a high heat for 2–3 minutes. Add a 120 g (4 oz) sachet oyster and spring onion stir-fry sauce and fry for a further 2–3 minutes or until the fish is cooked through and piping hot. Serve immediately with steamed rice.

Spicy Monkfish and Mixed Pepper Skewers Cut 700 g (1½ lb) monkfish fillets into bite-sized pieces and put in a non-reactive bowl. Stir in 1 tablespoon medium curry paste, 6 tablespoons coconut cream and the juice of 1 lime and season well. Cover and leave to marinate for 10–15 minutes. Meanwhile, core, deseed and cut 2 red peppers and 1 yellow pepper into bite-sized pieces. Thread the monkfish on to 8 metal skewers, alternating with the peppers. Cook under a preheated medium-hot grill for 4–5 minutes on each side or until the fish is cooked through. Serve with a green salad.

 # Spicy Prawn and Tomato Curry

Serves 4

2 tablespoons hot curry powder

1 teaspoon ground turmeric

4 garlic cloves, crushed

2 teaspoons peeled and finely grated fresh root ginger

2 tablespoons ground cumin

6 tablespoons tomato purée

1 teaspoon caster sugar or grated palm sugar

400 ml (14 fl oz) water

2 teaspoons tamarind paste

300 ml (½ pint) canned coconut milk

800 g (1¾ lb) raw tiger prawns, peeled and deveined, with tails left on

200 g (7 oz) cherry tomatoes

salt and pepper

chopped coriander leaves, to garnish

warm naan bread, to serve

- Put the curry powder, turmeric, garlic, ginger, cumin, tomato purée, sugar and measurement water in a heavy-based saucepan and mix together. Place over a high heat and bring to the boil. Cover, reduce the heat to low and simmer gently for 8–10 minutes.

- Increase the heat to high, stir in the tamarind paste and coconut milk and bring back to the boil. Add the prawns and cherry tomatoes and cook, uncovered, for 4–5 minutes or until the prawns turn pink and are completely cooked through. Season well.

- Ladle into warm bowls, scatter with chopped coriander leaves and serve with warm naan bread.

 ### Spicy Prawn and Tomato Salad

Arrange 500 g (1 lb) cooked peeled prawns, 4 sliced tomatoes and the leaves of 2 Baby Gem lettuces in a large salad bowl. Mix together 1 tablespoon medium curry powder, 6 tablespoons mayonnaise, the juice of 1 lemon and 5 tablespoons natural yogurt in a bowl, then season. Drizzle the dressing over the salad, toss to mix well and serve with crusty bread or warm naan bread.

 ### Spicy Prawn and Tomato Gratin

Heat 2 tablespoons sunflower oil in a large frying pan, add 2 finely chopped onions and cook over a medium-low heat, stirring occasionally, for 10 minutes until softened and lightly browned. Add 2 chopped garlic cloves, 1 deseeded and chopped green chilli, 1 tablespoon medium curry powder and 1 teaspoon grated fresh root ginger and fry, stirring, for 1–2 minutes, then add 400 g (13 oz) halved cherry tomatoes and cook, stirring occasionally, for 4–5 minutes until the tomatoes have softened. Remove from the heat and stir in 500 g (1 lb) raw peeled tiger prawns. Transfer to a shallow gratin dish, season and cook under a medium-hot grill for 5–6 minutes or until the prawns turn pink and are cooked through. Scatter over a small handful of chopped coriander leaves and serve with lemon wedges to squeeze over.

Tandoori King Prawn Skewers with Mint and Yogurt Dip

Serves 4

800 g (1¾ lb) raw unpeeled king prawns
3 tablespoons tandoori paste
6 tablespoons natural yogurt
juice of 2 limes
salt and pepper
lime wedges, to serve

For the dip

1 tablespoon mint jelly
2 tablespoons finely chopped mint leaves
1 tablespoon lime juice
200 g (7 oz) natural yogurt

- Put the prawns in a large non-reactive bowl. Mix together the tandoori paste, yogurt and lime juice in a bowl, then season well. Pour over the prawns and toss to coat evenly, then cover and leave to marinate for 8–10 minutes.

- Meanwhile, make the mint and yogurt dip. Mix together all the ingredients in a bowl until smooth, then season to taste. Cover and chill until ready to serve.

- Thread each prawn on to a small metal skewer, then cook under a preheated medium-hot grill for 6–8 minutes, turning once, or until the prawns turn pink and are cooked through.

- Transfer the skewers on to 4 serving plates and serve with the dip and lime wedges to squeeze over.

 Tandoori Prawn Stir-Fry

Heat 2 tablespoons sunflower oil in a large wok or frying pan until hot, add 2 tablespoons tandoori paste and 800 g (1¾ lb) raw peeled king or tiger prawns, season with salt and stir-fry over a high heat for 3–4 minutes or until the prawns turn pink and are cooked through. Remove from the heat, stir in the juice of 1 lemon and serve immediately with steamed rice or warm naan bread.

 Tandoori Prawn Biryani

Mix together 6 tablespoons natural yogurt and 2 tablespoons tandoori paste in a large bowl, add 600 g (1 lb 5 oz) raw peeled tiger prawns, then season and stir to mix well. Heat 2 tablespoons sunflower oil in a heavy-based saucepan, add 6 tablespoons shop-bought crispy onions, 450 g (14½ oz) basmati rice, 1 cinnamon stick, 6 cardamom pods, 2 cloves and 1 tablespoon cumin seeds and stir to mix well, then add the prawn mixture and stir to coat evenly. Pour over 800 ml (1 pint 8 fl oz) hot vegetable or fish stock, season with salt and bring to the boil. Cover tightly, reduce the heat to low and cook, undisturbed, for 15–20 minutes or until all the liquid is absorbed, the rice is tender and the prawns are cooked through. Remove from the heat and leave to stand for a few minutes before serving.

30 Thai Fish Ball Curry

Serves 4

1 tablespoon sunflower oil
1 tablespoon Thai red curry paste
600 ml (1 pint) canned coconut milk
2 teaspoons caster sugar
4 kaffir lime leaves, finely shredded
2 cm (¾ inch) length of trimmed
    lemon grass stalk, finely chopped
2 teaspoons fish sauce
1 carrot, cut into thin matchsticks
150 g (5 oz) mangetout, halved
    lengthways
steamed jasmine rice, to serve

For the fish balls

800 g (1¾ lb) firm white fish fillets,
    skinned and boned
2 garlic cloves, crushed
2 tablespoons cornflour
2 tablespoons dark soy sauce
2 tablespoons chopped coriander
1 teaspoon grated fresh root ginger

To garnish

sliced red chilli
coriander leaves

- To make the fish balls, put all the ingredients in a food processor or blender and blend until fairly smooth. Roll the mixture into bite-sized balls.

- Heat the oil in a large wok or heavy-based saucepan until hot, add the curry paste and stir-fry over a medium heat for 1–2 minutes, then add the coconut milk. Bring to the boil, then reduce the heat to low and simmer gently, uncovered, for 6–8 minutes.

- Add the fish balls, sugar, lime leaves, lemon grass, fish sauce, carrot and mangetout and bring back to the boil. Reduce the heat to low and simmer, uncovered, for 10–12 minutes or until the fish balls are cooked through.

- Ladle into warm bowls, scatter with sliced red chilli and coriander leaves and serve with steamed jasmine rice.

 Quick Thai Fish Ball Soup

Put 2 x 400 g (13 oz) cans vegetable soup, 2 teaspoons Thai red curry paste and 400 g (13 oz) ready-cooked fish balls (available from Oriental or Thai food stores) in a saucepan and bring to the boil, then reduce the heat to medium and cook for 3–4 minutes or until piping hot. Serve immediately.

Thai Fish Ball Noodles

Heat 2 tablespoons sunflower oil in a large wok or frying pan until hot, add 400 g (13 oz) ready-cooked fish balls (available from Oriental or Thai food stores) and stir-fry over a high heat for 4–5 minutes until browned. Add 1 tablespoon Thai red curry paste and 200 ml (7 fl oz) canned coconut milk and stir-fry for a further 2–3 minutes, then add a 300 g (10 oz) pack ready-prepared stir-fry vegetables and a 300 g (10 oz) bag fresh rice noodles. Toss to mix well, bring to the boil and cook for 2–3 minutes or until piping hot. Season, then serve immediately.

 Spiced Crayfish and Rocket Sandwiches

Serves 4

200 g (7 oz) mayonnaise
1 tablespoon mild curry powder
8 thick slices wholemeal bread
small handful of rocket leaves
400 g shop-bought ready-
cooked crayfish meat

To serve

crisps
salad (optional)

- Mix together the mayonnaise and curry powder in a bowl, then spread on to 8 thick slices of wholemeal bread.

- Top 4 of the slices with a small handful of rocket leaves and add a quarter of the crayfish meat each.

- Sandwich the remaining slices over the crayfish and press lightly to secure. Serve with crisps and a salad, if liked.

 Crayfish, Vegetable and Coconut Stir-Fry Heat 2 tablespoons sunflower oil in a large wok until hot, add 6 sliced spring onions, 2 chopped garlic cloves, 1 teaspoon peeled and grated fresh root ginger, 1 teaspoon medium curry powder, 1 deseeded and sliced red chilli and stir-fry for 2–3 minutes over a high heat. Add a 400 g (13 oz) pack ready-prepared stir-fry vegetables and stir-fry for a further 5–6 minutes. Add 200 ml (7 fl oz) coconut cream and 400 g (13 oz) shop-bought ready-cooked crayfish meat and continue to stir-fry for 4–5 minutes or until piping hot. Season and serve with noodles or rice.

Caribbean Crayfish and Coconut Curry Heat 2 tablespoons sunflower oil in a large frying pan, add 1 finely chopped onion, 2 crushed garlic cloves, 1 deseeded and finely chopped Scotch bonnet chilli and 1 tablespoon thyme and cook over a medium heat for about 5 minutes until the onion is softened. Stir in 1 tablespoon mild curry powder and cook for 1 minute until fragrant, then add 1 cored, deseeded and diced red pepper, 6 finely sliced spring onions and 200 g (7 oz) canned chopped tomatoes and cook for a further 2 minutes. Pour in a 400 ml (14 fl oz) can coconut milk and bring to the boil.

Reduce the heat slightly, then simmer for 6–8 minutes. Add 500 g (1 lb) shop-bought ready-cooked fresh crayfish meat and cook for 4–5 minutes until heated through, then season. Ladle into bowls and serve with bread or steamed rice.

Coconut Spiced Clams

Serves 4

4 tablespoons vegetable oil

2 shallots, very finely chopped

1 red chilli, slit lengthways and deseeded

3 cm (1 inch) piece of fresh root ginger, peeled and shredded

2 garlic cloves, finely chopped

2 plum tomatoes, finely chopped

1 tablespoon medium or hot curry powder

200 ml (7 fl oz) canned coconut milk

800 g (1¾ lb) fresh clams, scrubbed

1 large handful of chopped coriander leaves

3 tablespoons grated fresh coconut

To serve (optional)

salad

crusty bread

- Heat the oil in a large wok or saucepan until hot, add the shallots, red chilli, ginger and garlic and stir-fry over a medium heat for 3–4 minutes. Increase the heat to high, stir in the tomatoes, curry powder and coconut milk and cook for a further 4–5 minutes.

- Add the clams to the pan, discarding any that have cracked or don't shut when tapped, stir to mix and cover tightly, then continue to cook over a high heat for 6–8 minutes until the clams have opened. Discard any that remain closed.

- Stir in the chopped coriander and sprinkle over the grated coconut. Ladle into bowls and serve immediately with a fresh salad and crusty bread to mop up the juices.

---

10 Spicy Clam Omelette

Whisk 4 eggs, 2 teaspoons hot curry powder and a handful of chopped coriander together in a bowl. Heat 2 tablespoons olive oil in a frying pan and add the egg mixture, swirling to coat evenly. Cook for 1–2 minutes then add 280 g canned clams, rinsed and drained, and fold over the sides of the omelette to enclose the filling. Flip to seal and cook for 1–2 minutes. Keep warm while you repeat the recipe, to make 2 omelettes in total. Divide each in two and serve each half with a crisp green salad.

30 Spicy Clam and Coconut Chowder

Heat 2 tablespoons sunflower oil in a heavy-based saucepan, add 1 chopped onion, 1 deseeded and chopped red chilli, 1 tablespoon medium or hot curry powder and 2 chopped garlic cloves and cook, stirring, for 2–3 minutes. Add 400 g (13 oz) peeled and finely diced potatoes, 200 ml (7 fl oz) canned coconut milk and 600 ml (1 pint) hot fish stock and bring to the boil, then reduce the heat to medium and cook, uncovered, for 12–15 minutes or until the potatoes are tender. Increase the heat to high, stir in 400 g (13 oz) fresh scrubbed clams, discarding any that are cracked or don't shut when tapped, cover tightly and bring to the boil, then cook for 4–5 minutes or until the clams have opened. Discard any that remain closed. Season, stir in a small handful of chopped coriander and serve immediately.

Creamy Spiced Lobster Tail

Serves 4

2 egg yolks, beaten

100 ml (3½ fl oz) double cream

30 g (1 oz) butter

2 tablespoons dry sherry

½ teaspoon salt

1 tablespoon medium curry powder

4 tablespoons finely chopped coriander leaves, plus extra leaves to garnish

450 g (14½ oz) cooked lobster tail meat, cut into bite-sized pieces

To serve

lemon wedges

steamed rice

- Whisk together the egg yolks and double cream in a small bowl until well blended. Melt the butter in a saucepan over a low heat, then stir in the egg mixture and sherry. Cook, stirring, for about 10–12 minutes or until the mixture thickens, but do not allow to boil.

- Remove from the heat, then stir in the salt, curry powder and coriander. Stir in the lobster, then return the pan to a low heat and cook gently until heated through.

- Spoon into warm bowls, scatter with coriander leaves and serve with lemon wedges to squeeze over and steamed rice.

10 Spicy Lobster Bisque

Heat 1 tablespoon butter in a saucepan, add 1 deseeded and finely chopped red chilli, 1 teaspoon garlic paste and 1 teaspoon ginger paste and fry, stirring, for 30 seconds. Add 2 x 400 g (13 oz) cans lobster bisque soup and bring to a boil, then reduce the heat to medium and cook for a few minutes or until piping hot. Stir in 4 tablespoons finely chopped coriander leaves and serve with warm ciabatta bread.

30 Spicy Lobster Gratin

Melt 50 g (2 oz) butter in a saucepan over a low heat, add 2 tablespoons plain flour and 2 tablespoons medium or hot curry powder and cook, stirring, for 1–2 minutes. Gradually whisk in 250 ml (8 fl oz) double cream and 100 ml (3½ fl oz) milk and cook, stirring continuously, for about 5 minutes or until thickened. Cut 500 g (1 lb) cooked lobster tail meat into large pieces and add to the pan. Toss to mix well, season and pour into a shallow casserole dish. Sprinkle over 200 g (7 oz) fresh white breadcrumbs and place in a preheated oven, 220°C (425°F), Gas Mark 7, for 15–20 minutes or until bubbling. Serve warm with a crisp green salad.

10 Goan Fried Fish

Serves 4

1 teaspoon ground turmeric
1 teaspoon ginger paste
1 teaspoon garlic paste
1 teaspoon chilli powder
1 teaspoon ground cumin
1 teaspoon ground coriander
juice of 2 lemons
4 skinless halibut steaks, about
    200 g (7 oz) each
4 tablespoons sunflower oil
green salad, to serve (optional)

- Mix together the ground spices and pastes in a bowl. Add the juice of 2 lemons and stir to mix well. Spread the mixture all over the fish and season well.

- Heat 4 tablespoons sunflower oil in a large frying pan, add the fish and fry over a medium-high heat for 2–3 minutes on each side or until just cooked through. Serve with a green salad, if liked.

Goan Fishcakes

Place 400 g (13 oz) skinless halibut fillets, boned, and 400 g (13 oz) raw peeled prawns in a food processor or blender. Add 1 tablespoon Goan curry paste and blitz until smooth. Using wet hands, shape the mixture into 12 cakes. Heat 2 tablespoons sunflower oil in a large frying pan, add the fishcakes and fry over a medium-high heat for 3–4 minutes on each side or until cooked through. Serve with steamed rice and a salad.

Goan Fish Curry

Heat 2 tablespoons sunflower oil in a large heavy-based saucepan, add 2 finely chopped onions and cook over a medium heat, stirring occasionally, for 1–2 minutes until beginning to soften. Add 1 tablespoon grated fresh root ginger, 4 crushed garlic cloves and 2 deseeded and finely sliced red chillies and cook, stirring, for 1–2 minutes. Add ¼ teaspoon ground turmeric, 2 teaspoons each ground coriander and cumin and 1 teaspoon chilli powder and cook, stirring, for a further 1–2 minutes until fragrant, then stir in 1 tablespoon tamarind paste, 200 ml (7 fl oz) canned coconut milk and 300 ml (½ pint) water and bring to the boil. Add 1 teaspoon soft brown sugar then reduce the heat to low and simmer gently, uncovered, for 12–15 minutes. Stir in 800 g (1¾ lb) skinless halibut fillets, boned and cut into bite-sized pieces, increase the heat to high and cook for 4–5 minutes or until just cooked through, then season. Ladle into warm bowls and serve with steamed rice, poppadums and pickles.

30 Hot, Sweet and Sour Salmon

Serves 4

1 tablespoon fish sauce
1 teaspoon grated palm sugar or
    caster sugar
2 lemon grass stalks, bruised
600 ml (1 pint) water
2 tablespoons lemon juice
1 tablespoon tamarind paste
200 g (7 oz) pineapple flesh, cut
    into bite-sized pieces
8 salmon steaks, about 75 g
    (3 oz) each
steamed rice, to serve

For the spice paste

2 garlic cloves
4 dried red chillies
1 teaspoon sea salt
1 teaspoon ground turmeric
4 cm (1½ inch) length of trimmed
    lemon grass stalk, finely chopped
40 g (1½ oz) shrimp paste

- To make the spice paste, put all the ingredients in a food processor or blender and combine, adding a little water if needed.

- Transfer the paste to a large saucepan and stir in the fish sauce, sugar, lemon grass stalks and 400 ml (14 fl oz) of the measurement water. Bring to the boil, then reduce the heat slightly and simmer, uncovered, for 8–10 minutes.

- Mix together the lemon juice, tamarind paste and remaining water in a small bowl, then add to the pan with the pineapple and stir to mix well. Add the salmon steaks and simmer gently for 8–10 minutes or until the fish is cooked through.

- Spoon into warm bowls and serve with steamed rice.

 Grilled Hot, Sweet and Sour Salmon

Mix together 1 teaspoon lemon grass paste, 1 teaspoon hot chilli sauce, 1 teaspoon tamarind paste and 2 teaspoons sweet chilli sauce in a bowl, then spread the mixture over 4 large salmon steaks. Cook under a preheated hot grill for 5–6 minutes or until just cooked through. Serve immediately with salad.

 Hot and Sour Fish Soup

Heat 1 tablespoon sunflower oil in a heavy-based saucepan, add 8 finely sliced spring onions and 1 chopped garlic clove and cook, stirring, for 1–2 minutes, then stir in 1 teaspoon medium curry powder, 1 teaspoon red chilli paste, 1 teaspoon lemon grass paste and 1 teaspoon tamarind paste and cook for a further 30 seconds. Pour in 600 ml (1 pint) hot fish stock and 400 ml (14 fl oz) canned coconut milk and bring to the boil, then cook, stirring, for 4–5 minutes. Add 400 g (13 oz) skinless salmon fillets, boned and cubed, and cook gently for 5–6 minutes or until the fish is just cooked through. Serve immediately.

HOT-FISH-BEC

30 Mustard and Curry Leaf Halibut

Serves 4

1 teaspoon ground turmeric
1 tablespoon chilli powder
2 tablespoons grated fresh coconut
4 tablespoons vegetable oil
1 teaspoon black mustard seeds
20 fresh curry leaves
2 onions, thinly sliced
4 green chillies, deseeded and sliced
2.5 cm (1 inch) piece of fresh root
   ginger, peeled and cut into
   matchsticks
6 garlic cloves, finely chopped
1 kg (2¼ lb) skinless halibut fillets,
   boned and cut into bite-sized
   pieces
400 ml (14 fl oz) can coconut milk
300 ml (½ pint) water
1 tablespoon tamarind paste
salt
steamed basmati rice, to serve

- Mix together the turmeric, chilli powder and coconut in a small bowl and set aside.

- Heat the oil in a large wok or heavy-based saucepan until hot, then add the mustard seeds and cook over a medium-high heat for a few minutes until the seeds begin to pop, then add the curry leaves, onions, green chillies, ginger and garlic and stir-fry for about 5 minutes until fragrant.

- Stir in the turmeric mixture and stir-fry for a further 1 minute. Add the fish, then stir in the coconut milk and measurement water. Finally, add the tamarind paste. Bring to the boil, then reduce the heat to low and simmer gently, uncovered, for 15 minutes or until the fish is cooked through. Season well with salt.

- Ladle into warm bowls and serve with steamed basmati rice, if liked.

 Pan-Fried Fish with Mustard and Curry Leaves Mix together 2 tablespoons wholegrain mustard, 6 crushed dried curry leaves, 1 teaspoon chilli powder and 1 teaspoon medium or hot curry powder in a bowl. Season with salt, then spread the mixture all over 4 skinless plaice fillets. Heat 2 tablespoons sunflower oil in a large frying pan and fry the fish fillets for 2–3 minutes on each side or until cooked through. Serve with a green salad.

 Baked Mustard and Curry Leaf Fish Mix together 1 tablespoon medium or hot curry paste, 4 tablespoons coconut cream, 2 tablespoons wholegrain mustard and the juice of 1 lemon in a bowl, then spread the mixture all over 4 thick, skinless halibut fillets. Arrange in a shallow ovenproof dish in a single layer, scatter over 10–12 fresh curry leaves and season. Place in a preheated oven, 220°C (425°F), Gas Mark 7, for 12–15 minutes or until the fish is cooked through. Serve with steamed vegetables and rice.

HOT-FISH-WYM

Prawn, Lemon Grass and Mango Curry

Serves 4

2 tablespoons vegetable oil

2 garlic cloves, finely chopped

2 shallots, thinly sliced

1 carrot, peeled and cut into thin matchsticks

8 cm (3 inch) length of trimmed lemon grass stalk, finely chopped

1 red chilli, deseeded and chopped

1 tablespoon hot curry powder

300 ml (½ pint) canned coconut milk

200 ml (7 fl oz) water

1 tablespoon fish sauce

1 kg (2¼ lb) raw king prawns, peeled and deveined, with tails left on

300 g (10 oz) mango flesh, cut into 1.5 cm (¾ inch) cubes

Thai basil leaves, to garnish

steamed jasmine rice, to serve

- Heat the oil in a heavy-based saucepan, add the garlic, shallots and carrot and cook over a medium heat, stirring occasionally, for 1–2 minutes until softened. Add the lemon grass, red chilli and curry powder and cook for a further 3 minutes or until fragrant.

- Pour in the coconut milk, measurement water and fish sauce and bring to a simmer. Cook for 5 minutes, then reduce the heat to medium-low, stir in the prawns and mango and simmer gently, partially covered, for 5 minutes or until the prawns turn pink and are cooked through.

- Ladle into warm bowls, scatter with Thai basil leaves and serve with steamed jasmine rice.

---

10 **Prawn, Lemon Grass and Mango Stir-Fry**

Heat 2 tablespoons sunflower oil in a large wok until hot, add 2 chopped shallots, 2 deseeded and chopped red chillies, 2 chopped garlic cloves and an 8 cm (3 inch) length of trimmed lemon grass stalk, finely chopped, and stir-fry over a high heat for 1 minute. Add 1 tablespoon hot curry powder, 600 g (1 lb 5 oz) cooked peeled prawns and the diced flesh of 1 ripe mango and stir-fry for a further 3–4 minutes or until piping hot. Serve with noodles.

30 **Prawn, Lemon Grass and Mango Rice**

Heat 2 tablespoons sunflower oil in a heavy-based saucepan, add 2 teaspoons cumin seeds, 2 cloves, 1 cinnamon stick, 2 chopped shallots, 2 deseeded and chopped red chillies and 2 chopped garlic cloves and cook, stirring, for 2–3 minutes. Add 1 tablespoon hot curry powder, 450 g (14½ fl oz) basmati rice and 1 tablespoon lemon grass paste and stir until the rice is well coated, then pour in 800 ml (1 pint 8 fl oz) hot vegetable stock and bring to the boil. Add 500 g (1 lb) raw peeled tiger prawns and the diced flesh of 1 ripe mango. Cover tightly, reduce the heat to low and cook, undisturbed, for 15–20 minutes or until the liquid is absorbed, the rice is tender and the prawns are cooked through. Remove from the heat and leave to stand in the pan for a few minutes before serving.

30 Scallop Molee

Serves 4

1 onion, coarsely grated
4 garlic cloves, crushed
2 green chillies, deseeded and
   finely chopped
1 tablespoon ground cumin
1 teaspoon ground coriander
1 teaspoon ground turmeric
30 g (1 oz) coriander leaves, finely
   chopped, plus extra to garnish
200 ml (7 fl oz) water
2 tablespoons sunflower oil
6 fresh curry leaves, plus extra
   to garnish
400 ml (14 fl oz) can coconut milk
700 g (1½ lb) king scallops,
   cleaned
salt and pepper
steamed basmati rice, to serve

- Put the onion, garlic, green chillies, ground spices, chopped coriander and measurement water in a food processor or blender and blend until smooth.

- Heat the oil in a large heavy-based frying pan, add the curry leaves and fry, stirring, for 20–30 seconds, then add the blended mixture, stir and cook over a high heat for 3–4 minutes. Reduce the heat to low, pour in the coconut milk and simmer gently, uncovered, for 12–15 minutes.

- Add the scallops to the pan, bring back to the boil, then reduce the heat to low and simmer gently for 2–3 minutes or until the scallops are just cooked through. Season well.

- Spoon into warm bowls, scatter with a few curry and coriander leaves and serve with steamed basmati rice.

---

1 **Pan-Fried Scallops with Chilli, Coriander and Coconut** Heat 2 tablespoons sunflower oil in a large frying pan, add 700 g (1½ lb) cleaned king scallops and cook over a high heat for 1 minute on each side. Transfer to warm serving plates, season and scatter over 1 deseeded and finely chopped red chilli and a large handful of chopped coriander. Drizzle over 4 tablespoons thinned coconut cream and serve.

2 **Scallop, Chilli and Coconut Pasta** Cook 375 g (12 oz) dried linguine in a large saucepan of salted boiling water according to the packet instructions until al dente. Meanwhile, heat 2 tablespoons sunflower oil in a large frying pan, add 500 g (1 lb) cleaned king scallops in a single layer and fry for 1 minute on each side. Transfer to a large dish and keep warm. Wipe out the pan and add 1 tablespoon sunflower oil. Stir in 1 deseeded and chopped red chilli and 2 chopped garlic cloves and fry, stirring, for 1–2 minutes. Remove from the heat and return the scallops to the pan with 100 ml (3½ fl oz) coconut cream and a handful of chopped coriander leaves. Drain the pasta, then add to the scallop mixture. Toss to mix well, season and serve.

Garlicky Chilli and Tomato Prawns

Serves 4

800 g (1¾ lb) raw king prawns, peeled and deveined, with tails left on

juice of 1 lime

1 teaspoon salt

2 tablespoons sunflower oil

1 onion, finely chopped

1 red chilli, deseeded and finely chopped

4 garlic cloves, finely chopped

2 teaspoons sweet smoked paprika

4 plum tomatoes, roughly chopped

2 teaspoons tomato purée

1 teaspoon caster sugar

chopped flat leaf parsley, to garnish

- Put the prawns in a non-reactive bowl and add the lime juice and salt. Set aside.

- Heat the oil in a large wok or frying pan until hot, add the onion, red chilli and garlic and stir-fry over a high heat for 1–2 minutes. Add the paprika and tomatoes and stir-fry for a further 1–2 minutes.

- Add the prawns and their reserved juices to the pan and continue to stir-fry for 3–4 minutes or until the prawns turn pink and are cooked through. Stir in the tomato purée and sugar and cook, stirring, for 1–2 minutes.

- Remove from the heat, scatter with chopped parsley and serve.

 Prawn, Tomato and Chilli Salad

Put 500 g (1 lb) cooked peeled prawns, the leaves from 2 Baby Gem lettuces and 400 g (13 oz) halved cherry tomatoes in a large salad bowl. Mix together 1 deseeded and finely chopped red chilli, 6 tablespoons extra-virgin olive oil, the juice of 1 lemon, 1 teaspoon runny honey and 1 teaspoon Dijon mustard in a bowl, then season. Pour the dressing over the salad, toss to mix well and serve.

 Chilli, Tomato and Prawn Gratin

Heat 1 tablespoon sunflower oil in a frying pan, add 1 chopped onion, 4 chopped garlic cloves and 1 deseeded and sliced red chilli and cook over a medium heat for 3–4 minutes until softened. Add a 400 g (13 oz) can chopped tomatoes and cook over a medium heat for 6–8 minutes or until thickened. Season, then spoon into a shallow ovenproof dish. Spoon over 800 g (1¾ lb) raw peeled tiger prawns, toss to mix well and cook under a preheated medium-hot grill for 5–6 minutes or until the prawns turn pink and are cooked through. Scatter with chopped flat leaf parsley and serve with crusty bread.

Sumac, Chilli and Lemon-Spiced Monkfish Skewers

Serves 4

800 g (1¾ lb) monkfish tail, cut into bite-sized pieces

3 lemons

2 tablespoons extra-virgin olive oil

2 teaspoons sumac

3 teaspoons dried red chilli flakes

4 garlic cloves, finely chopped

1 red chilli, deseeded and finely chopped

35 g (1½ oz) flat leaf parsley, finely chopped

salt and pepper

rocket salad, to serve

· Put the fish in a large non-reactive bowl. Finely grate 2 of the lemons and set aside the grated rind. Halve the grated lemons and squeeze the juice over the fish.

· Add the oil, sumac and chilli flakes to the fish mixture, season well with salt and toss to coat evenly. Cover and leave to marinate until ready to cook.

· Mix together the reserved lemon rind, garlic, chopped red chilli and parsley in a bowl. Season well and set aside.

· Cut the remaining lemon into thin slices. Thread the monkfish on to 8 long metal skewers, alternating with the lemon slices. Cook under a preheated hot grill for 4–5 minutes on each side or until the fish is cooked through.

· Transfer the skewers on to 4 serving plates, sprinkle over the lemon rind mixture and serve with a rocket salad.

 Sumac and Chilli Fish Butties with Lemon Mayo Poach 500 g (1 lb) skinless cod fillets in a saucepan of simmering water for 4–5 minutes or until cooked through. Meanwhile, halve 4 warm rolls and thickly spread each half with shop-bought lemon mayonnaise. Lightly sprinkle each half with a little sumac and chilli powder. Flake the poached fish with a fork, removing any bones, then divide between the roll bases. Spoon 1 tablespoon sweet chilli sauce over each and top with the roll lids. Serve with fries and a salad.

 Sumac and Lemon Monkfish Stew Heat 2 tablespoons sunflower oil in a heavy-based saucepan, add 1 chopped onion, 2 chopped garlic cloves, 1 tablespoon mild curry powder and 1 cinnamon stick and cook over a medium heat, stirring occasionally, for 3–4 minutes until the onion is softened. Add 600 g (1 lb 5 oz) monkfish tail, thickly sliced, and cook for a further 1–2 minutes. Stir in 500 ml (17 fl oz) hot fish stock and bring to the boil, then reduce the heat to low and simmer gently, uncovered, for 12–15 minutes. Add 2 tablespoons chopped preserved lemon, remove from the heat and sprinkle over 1 teaspoon sumac and a small handful of chopped flat leaf parsley. Serve with couscous or steamed rice.

30 Yellow Fish, Potato and Tomato Curry

Serves 4

2 tablespoons sunflower oil
1 onion, finely chopped
1 tablespoon ground turmeric
400 ml (14 fl oz) can coconut milk
200 ml (7 fl oz) water
2 potatoes, peeled and cubed
800 g (1¾ lb) thick skinless salmon
   fillets, boned and cut into chunks
2 tomatoes, roughly chopped
salt
chopped coriander, to garnish

For the spice paste

3 teaspoons garlic paste
1 teaspoon ginger paste
2 green chillies, deseeded and
   finely chopped
2 teaspoons grated fresh root ginger

To serve

steamed rice
lime wedges
chopped red chilli

- To make the spice paste, pound together all the ingredients using a small pestle and mortar until you have a fairly smooth paste. Alternatively, whizz in a mini food processor.

- Heat the oil in a large wok or heavy-based saucepan until hot, add the spice paste and stir-fry over a medium heat for 30–40 seconds, then add the onion and turmeric and stir-fry for a further 2–3 minutes until fragrant.

- Pour in the coconut milk and measurement water, then stir in the potatoes. Bring to the boil, then reduce the heat to low and simmer gently, uncovered, for 10–12 minutes, stirring occasionally.

- Season the fish with salt, then add to the pan with the tomatoes and bring back to the boil. Reduce the heat to medium-low and simmer gently for 6–8 minutes until the fish is cooked through.

- Ladle into warm bowls, scatter with chopped coriander and serve with steamed rice, lime wedges and chopped red chilli.

 Spicy Fish and Tomato Soup

Heat 1 tablespoon sunflower oil in a saucepan, add 1 tablespoon mild curry paste and fry, stirring, for 20–30 seconds. Add 2 x 400 g (13 oz) cans cream of tomato soup and bring to the boil, then reduce the heat to medium, stir in 400 g (13 oz) flaked hot-smoked salmon fillets, bones removed, and cook for a few minutes or until piping hot. Serve with crusty bread.

 Spicy Yellow Fish and Tomato Rice

Poach 3 skinless salmon fillets in a saucepan of simmering water for 4–5 minutes until cooked through, then flake into large pieces, removing any bones. Meanwhile, heat 1 tablespoon sunflower oil in a large frying pan until hot, add 1 chopped onion and stir-fry over a high heat, stirring occasionally, for 3–4 minutes until softened. Add 1 teaspoon cumin seeds, ½ teaspoon ground turmeric, 2 teaspoons hot curry powder, 1 teaspoon ginger paste and 1 teaspoon garlic paste and stir-fry for a further 2–3 minutes, then add 500 g (1 lb) shop-bought ready-cooked basmati rice and 100 ml (3½ fl oz) canned coconut milk. Stir, then cook for 6–8 minutes or until piping hot and the liquid is almost absorbed. Add the poached salmon with 2 diced plum tomatoes, toss to mix well, season and serve.

HOT-FISH-KEY

30 Turmeric Mackerel Skewers with Chilli Rice Noodles

Serves 4

4 large boned mackerel fillets,
about 200 g (7 oz) each,
trimmed and cleaned
½ teaspoon ground turmeric
1 tablespoon mild curry paste
juice of 2 lemons
1 tablespoon sunflower oil
salt and pepper

For the noodles

200 g (7 oz) dried rice noodles
1 tablespoon vegetable oil
1 red chilli, deseeded and finely
sliced
6 spring onions, finely shredded
4 tablespoons roughly chopped
mint, plus extra to garnish
4 tablespoons roughly chopped
coriander leaves
3 tablespoons chilli-roasted
peanuts, roughly chopped

- Put the fish fillets in a large, non-reactive shallow dish. Mix together the turmeric, curry paste, lemon juice and sunflower oil and pour over the fish. Season, then toss to mix well and set aside.

- Put the rice noodles in a heatproof bowl and pour over boiling water to cover. Leave to soak for 3–4 minutes, then drain and refresh under cold running water. Drain again and set aside.

- Thread 2 metal skewers through each fish fillet to keep them flattened while cooking, then place under a preheated medium-high grill for 6–8 minutes or until just cooked through.

- Meanwhile, heat the vegetable oil in a large wok or frying pan until hot, add the chilli, spring onions and drained noodles and stir-fry over a high heat for 2–3 minutes or until piping hot, then stir in the mint and coriander and season.

- Divide the noodles on to warm serving plates or into shallow bowls. Top each with the grilled fish and scatter over the chopped chilli-roasted peanuts. Scatter with extra chopped mint and serve immediately.

 Mackerel and Rice Noodle Stir-Fry

Heat 2 tablespoons sunflower oil in a large wok or frying pan. Add 2 x 300 g packs fresh cooked rice noodles and a 120 g sachet sweet chilli stir-fry sauce. Stir-fry for 3–4 minutes or until piping hot. Remove from the heat and flake in 4 smoked mackerel fillets and 6 sliced spring onions. Toss to mix well and serve immediately.

 Turmeric Mackerel Curry

Heat 1 tablespoon sunflower oil in a large saucepan, add 1 chopped onion, 1 teaspoon turmeric and 1 tablespoon mild curry powder and fry, stirring, for 3–4 minutes until softened. Add 1 teaspoon ginger paste and 1 teaspoon garlic paste and fry for a further 30–40 seconds, then pour in a 400 ml (14 fl oz) can coconut milk and 100 ml (3½ fl oz) hot fish stock. Bring to the boil, then add 4 large boned mackerel fillets, about 200 g (7 oz) each, trimmed and cleaned, and cook over a medium heat for 8–10 minutes or until the fish is cooked through. Season, then serve with basmati rice.

QuickCook
Vegetarian

Recipes listed by cooking time

10

30 Aubergine, Tomato and Chilli Curry

Serves 4

2 large aubergines

100 ml (3½ fl oz) vegetable oil

2 onions, very thinly sliced

6 garlic cloves, finely chopped

3 teaspoons peeled and grated finely chopped fresh root ginger

2 red chillies, deseeded and thinly sliced

200 g (7 oz) canned chopped tomatoes

6 kaffir lime leaves

1 tablespoon kecap manis (thick soy sauce)

2 tablespoons dark soy sauce

1 teaspoon soft light brown sugar

juice of 1 lime

small handful of chopped coriander leaves

2 tablespoons chopped roasted peanuts

steamed rice or rice noodles, to serve

- Cut the aubergines into finger-thick batons. Reserve 1 tablespoon of the oil, then heat the remaining oil in a large frying pan, add the aubergines and fry over a medium heat, stirring occasionally, for 5–6 minutes or until lightly browned. Remove with a slotted spoon and drain on kitchen paper.

- Heat the reserved oil in the pan, add the onions and garlic and cook over a medium heat, stirring occasionally, for 6–7 minutes until softened and lightly browned. Add the ginger, red chillies, tomatoes and lime leaves and cook for 2–3 minutes, stirring frequently. Return the aubergines to the pan with a splash of water and simmer gently for 2–3 minutes.

- Remove from the heat and stir in the kecap manis, soy sauce, sugar, lime juice and chopped coriander.

- Spoon into warm bowls, sprinkle over the chopped peanuts and serve with steamed rice or rice noodles.

 Aubergine, Tomato and Chilli Salad

Drain 400 g (13 oz) chargrilled aubergines in olive oil from a jar, reserving the oil, and put the aubergines in a salad bowl with 8 sliced plum tomatoes and a handful of rocket leaves. Mix 6 tablespoons of the reserved oil, the juice of 2 lemons and 1 teaspoon chilli paste in a bowl, then season. Pour the dressing over the salad, toss to mix well and serve with crusty bread.

 Chilli, Aubergine and Tomato Sauté

Cut 2 aubergines into 1.5 cm (¾ inch) cubes. Heat 2 tablespoons sunflower oil in a large frying pan, add the aubergines and fry over a medium heat, stirring occasionally, for 6–8 minutes or until lightly browned on all sides. Stir in 1 finely chopped onion, 2 chopped garlic cloves, 2 deseeded and sliced red chillies and 2 teaspoons cumin seeds and cook for a further for 4–5 minutes. Add 4 chopped plum tomatoes, season and heat through until piping hot. Serve with steamed rice or bread.

30 Chilli, Cherry Tomato and Goats' Cheese Tart

Serves 4

375 g (12 oz) ready-rolled
  puff pastry
flour, for dusting
8 tablespoons chilli jam
400 g (13 oz) mixed red and
  yellow cherry tomatoes, halved
200 g (7 oz) soft goats' cheese
4 tablespoons finely chopped
  mint leaves, to garnish
rocket salad, to serve (optional)

- Unroll the puff pastry on to a lightly floured work surface and cut into a 30 x 20 cm (12 x 8 inch) rectangle. Using a sharp knife, score a border 2 cm (¾ inch) from the edge of the pastry. Put the pastry on a baking sheet and place in a preheated oven, 220°C (425°F), Gas Mark 7, for 10–12 minutes or until the pastry has risen and is cooked through and lightly golden. Cool for 5 minutes.

- Spoon the chilli jam evenly over the base of the puff pastry case, then top with the tomatoes. Crumble over the goats' cheese and return the filled tart to the oven for 6–8 minutes or until the cheese has melted and the tart has heated through.

- Scatter over the chopped mint and serve with a rocket salad, if liked.

10 Chilli, Cherry Tomato and Goats' Cheese

Salad Halve 500 g (1 lb) mixed red and yellow cherry tomatoes and put in a large serving dish, then crumble over 200 g (7 oz) soft goats' cheese. Mix together 6 tablespoons extra-virgin olive oil, 1 deseeded and finely chopped red chilli, 3 tablespoons red wine vinegar, 1 teaspoon runny honey and 1 teaspoon Dijon mustard in a bowl, then season. Drizzle the dressing over the tomato and goats' cheese. Scatter over a small handful of mint leaves and serve.

20 Chilli, Cherry Tomato and Goats' Cheese Pasta

Cook 375 g (12 oz) dried penne in a saucepan of salted boiling water according to the packet instructions until al dente. Meanwhile, heat 4 tablespoons olive oil in a large frying pan, add 2 finely chopped shallots and cook over a medium heat, stirring occasionally, for 6–8 minutes until softened. Add 3 chopped garlic cloves, 1 deseeded and finely chopped red chilli and 300 g (10 oz) halved mixed red and yellow cherry tomatoes and cook, stirring, for a further 2–3 minutes. Drain the pasta, then add to the pan with 200 g (7 oz) crumbled soft goats' cheese and season. Serve immediately.

HOT-VEGE-HOA

30 Creamy Beetroot, Green Bean and Tomato Curry

Serves 4

2 tablespoons sunflower oil

1 teaspoon black mustard seeds

1 onion, chopped

2 garlic cloves, chopped

2 red chillies, deseeded and finely chopped

10–12 fresh curry leaves

1 teaspoon ground turmeric

1 teaspoon cumin seeds

1 cinnamon stick

400 g (13 oz) raw beetroot, peeled and cut into matchsticks

200 g (7 oz) green beans, trimmed

6 plum tomatoes, chopped

250 ml (8 fl oz) water

100 ml (3½ fl oz) canned coconut milk

juice of 1 lime

salt and pepper

chopped coriander, to garnish

- Heat the oil in a large heavy-based saucepan until hot, then add the mustard seeds and cook over a medium heat for a few minutes until the seeds begin to pop, then add the onion, garlic and red chillies and cook, stirring occasionally, for 5 minutes until the onion is soft and translucent.

- Add the remaining spices, the beetroot and green beans and cook for a further 1–2 minutes. Stir in the tomatoes and measurement water and simmer, uncovered, stirring occasionally, for 15–20 minutes or until the beetroot is tender.

- Pour in the coconut milk and simmer for a further 1–2 minutes, then stir in the lime juice and season to taste. Ladle into warm bowls, scatter with chopped coriander and serve.

---

10 Curried Beetroot, Green Bean and Tomato Broth

Put 400 g (13 oz) ready-cooked fresh beetroot, diced, in a blender and whizz until fairly chunky. Transfer to a saucepan and stir in 300 ml (½ pint) canned coconut milk, a 600 g (1 lb 5 oz) pot fresh tomato soup, 200 g (7 oz) finely chopped green beans and 2 teaspoons mild curry paste. Bring to the boil, then reduce the heat to medium and cook for 3–4 minutes or until piping hot. Sprinkle with 100 g (3½ oz) croûtons and serve.

20 Curried Beetroot, Green Bean and Tomato Rice

Heat 1 tablespoon butter and 1 tablespoon olive oil in a large frying pan, add 1 chopped red onion, 300 g (10 oz) finely diced shop-bought ready-cooked fresh beetroot, 300 g (10 oz) finely sliced trimmed green beans and 1 tablespoon medium or hot curry powder and cook, stirring, for 2–3 minutes until softened. Add a 400 g (13 oz) can chopped tomatoes and bring to the boil, then cook for 6–8 minutes or until slightly thickened. Stir in 500 g (1 lb) shop-bought ready-cooked long-grain rice and continue to cook for 5–6 minutes or until piping hot. Season, stir in 4 tablespoons crème fraîche and serve at once.

HOT-VEGE-DAE

30 Mango and Coconut Curry

Serves 4

4 firm ripe mangoes, peeled, stoned and cut into bite-sized pieces
1 teaspoon ground turmeric
1 teaspoon chilli powder
250 ml (8 fl oz) water
300 ml (½ pint) natural yogurt, lightly whisked
4 tablespoons sunflower oil
2 teaspoons black mustard seeds
3–4 hot dried red chillies
10–12 fresh curry leaves
steamed rice, to serve (optional)

For the coconut paste

350 g (11½ oz) grated fresh coconut
3–4 green chillies, deseeded and roughly chopped
1 tablespoon cumin seeds
250 ml (8 fl oz) water

- To make the coconut paste, put all the ingredients in a food processor or blender and blend to a fine paste.

- Put the mangoes in a heavy-based saucepan, add the turmeric, chilli powder and measurement water and bring to the boil, then remove from the heat.

- Add the coconut paste to the mango mixture. Stir to mix well, then cover, return to a medium heat and simmer for 10–12 minutes, stirring occasionally. Add the yogurt and heat gently, stirring continuously, until just warmed through (do not let the mixture boil or it will curdle). Remove from the heat and keep warm.

- Heat the oil in a small frying pan until hot, then add the mustard seeds and cook over a medium-high heat for a few minutes until the seeds begin to pop, then add the dried chillies and curry leaves and stir-fry for a few seconds until the chillies darken. Pour the oil mixture into the mango curry and stir in gently.

- Ladle into warm bowls and serve with steamed rice, if liked.

 Spiced Mango and Coconut Salad

Slice 4 ripe peeled and stoned mangoes and arrange on a large serving plate. Sprinkle over 100 g (3½ oz) grated fresh coconut. Meanwhile, heat 6 tablespoons sunflower oil in a small frying pan until hot, add 2 teaspoons black mustard seeds and cook over a medium-high heat for a few minutes until the seeds begin to pop, then add 1 teaspoon cumin seeds, 1 dried red chilli and 10 fresh curry leaves and stir-fry for a few seconds until the chilli darkens. Remove from the heat and drizzle the oil over the mango and coconut. Toss to mix well and serve.

 Spicy Mango and Coconut Rice

Cook 400 g (13 oz) basmati rice in a large saucepan of lightly salted boiling water for 10–12 minutes or until just tender. Drain well, then put in a large bowl. Peel, stone and cut 2 mangoes into bite-sized pieces, then stir into the rice with a large handful of chopped coriander, 1 deseeded and finely chopped red chilli and 100 g (3½ oz) grated fresh coconut. Season and serve warm or at room temperature.

30 Island-Spiced Sweetcorn with Avocado and Tomato

Serves 4

2 sweetcorn cobs

3 tablespoons sunflower oil

1 red pepper, halved lengthways, cored and deseeded

1 avocado

½ Scotch bonnet chilli or hot red chilli, deseeded and finely chopped

6 plum tomatoes, roughly chopped

1 small bunch of coriander leaves, roughly chopped

juice of 2 limes

140 ml (¼ pint) extra-virgin olive oil

salt and pepper

warm flatbreads, to serve

- Blanch the corn cobs in a large saucepan of boiling water for 30–45 seconds. Drain, then brush with the sunflower oil and cook under a grill preheated to its highest setting for 4–5 minutes, turning frequently, until beginning to char at the edges. Using a sharp knife, cut the kernels from the cobs and put in a large bowl.

- Meanwhile, cook the red pepper halves, skin-side up, under the preheated grill for 6–8 minutes until the skin begins to blister. Place in a plastic food bag, seal and leave for 5 minutes. When cool, peel away the blackened skin, then dice the flesh and add to the bowl of sweetcorn.

- Halve, peel and stone the avocado, then dice the flesh. Stir into the sweetcorn mixture with the chilli and tomatoes.

- In a separate bowl, mix together the coriander, lime juice and olive oil, then season and whisk well. Pour the dressing over the sweetcorn mixture and toss through gently. Serve with warm flatbreads.

 Spicy Sweetcorn, Avocado and Tomato Salad Tip a drained 340 g (11½ oz) can sweetcorn kernels into a large salad bowl, then add 1 deseeded and finely chopped red chilli, 4 chopped tomatoes and 2 peeled, stoned and diced avocados. Pour over 150 ml (¼ pint) Thai ginger and chilli salad dressing. Season, toss to mix well and serve.

 Spicy Sweetcorn, Avocado and Tomato Pasta Cook 375 g (12 oz) dried penne in a large saucepan of salted boiling water according to the packet instructions until al dente. Meanwhile, heat 2 tablespoons olive oil in a large saucepan, add 1 chopped garlic clove, 1 deseeded and finely chopped red chilli and 6 sliced spring onions and cook over a medium heat, stirring, for 2–3 minutes. Stir in 3 diced plum tomatoes and a drained 340 g (11½ oz) can sweetcorn kernels and cook for a further 6–8 minutes or until piping hot. Drain the pasta, then add to the sweetcorn with 2 peeled, stoned and diced avocados. Season, toss to mix well and serve scattered with chopped coriander.

30 Sweet Potato and Lychee Curry

Serves 4

350 g (11½ oz)jasmine rice, rinsed
1 tablespoon sunflower oil
3 tablespoons Thai red curry paste
1 teaspoon peeled and finely
    grated fresh root ginger
finely grated rind of 1 lime
400 ml (14 fl oz) hot
    vegetable stock
200 ml (7 fl oz) coconut cream
400 g (13 oz) can lychees, drained
    and syrup reserved
2 sweet potatoes, peeled and cut
    into bite-sized pieces
2 tablespoons fish sauce

To garnish

4 kaffir lime leaves, finely
    shredded
1 red chilli, deseeded and finely
    sliced lengthways

- Cook the rice in a large heavy-based saucepan of lightly salted boiling water, covered tightly, for 15–20 minutes or until just tender. Drain well and set aside.

- Meanwhile, heat the oil in a large wok or frying pan until hot, add the curry paste, ginger and lime rind and stir-fry over a medium heat for 1 minute or until fragrant.

- Pour over the stock and coconut cream, stir until well blended and bring to the boil. Add the lychees and sweet potatoes, reduce the heat to medium and simmer for 10–15 minutes or until the sweet potatoes are tender. Add 5 tablespoons of the reserved lychee syrup and the fish sauce and stir through.

- Ladle into warm bowls and scatter with the lime leaves and thin strips of chilli. Serve with the steamed jasmine rice.

 Spicy Sweet Potato and Lychee Salad
Put 400 g (13 oz) cooked sweet potato cubes, a drained 400 g (13 oz) can lychees and a 80 g (3 oz) bag mixed salad leaves in a large salad bowl. Mix together 4 tablespoons light olive oil, ½ teaspoon Thai red curry paste, 6 tablespoons coconut cream, 1 teaspoon grated palm sugar or caster sugar and the juice of 1 lime in a small bowl, then season. Pour the dressing over the salad, toss to mix well and serve.

 Spicy Sweet Potato and Lychee Noodles
Heat 2 tablespoons sunflower oil in a large wok or frying pan until hot, add 2 tablespoons Thai red curry paste, 400 g (13 oz) peeled and finely diced sweet potato and 8 sliced spring onions and stir-fry over a high heat for 1–2 minutes, then add 300 ml (½ pint) hot vegetable stock and bring to the boil. Reduce the heat to medium and cook for 8–10 minutes or until the sweet potatoes are tender.

Stir in 100 ml (3½ fl oz) coconut cream and a 300 g (10 oz) bag fresh egg noodles and bring back to the boil. Add a drained 400g (13 oz) can lychees and cook gently for 3–4 minutes or until piping hot. Season well, then serve.

30 Moroccan Vegetable Tagine with Couscous

Serves 4

200 g (7 oz) couscous
550 ml (18 fl oz) boiling water
2 tablespoons sunflower oil
1 large onion, finely chopped
2 garlic cloves, minced
1 teaspoon grated fresh root ginger
2 teaspoons ground cumin
1 teaspoon ground coriander
2 teaspoon ground cinnamon
1 teaspoon ground turmeric
2 teaspoons dried red chilli flakes
1 tablespoon harissa paste
400 g (13 oz) can chopped tomatoes
250 ml (8 fl oz) hot vegetable stock
2 red peppers, cored, deseeded
  and cut into bite-sized pieces
700 g (1½ lb) butternut squash,
  peeled, deseeded and cubed
100 g (3½ oz) golden sultanas
salt and pepper
chopped coriander, to garnish

- Put the couscous in a large heatproof bowl and season with salt. Pour over the measurement water, cover with clingfilm and leave to stand for 10 minutes, or according to the packet instructions, until the water is absorbed. Gently fork to separate the grains, then set aside and keep warm.

- Meanwhile, heat the oil in a large frying pan, add the onion and cook over a medium heat, stirring occasionally, for 2–3 minutes until softened. Add the garlic, ginger, ground spices, chilli flakes, harissa, tomatoes and stock and bring to the boil, then reduce the heat to low, cover and simmer gently for 10–12 minutes.

- Stir in the red peppers, squash and sultanas, re-cover and increase the heat to medium. Simmer for 10–15 minutes or until the vegetables are tender, then season to taste.

- Spoon the couscous into warm bowls, then ladle over the tagine and serve scattered with chopped coriander.

 Moroccan Couscous Salad

Put 250 g (8 oz) couscous in a large heatproof bowl and pour over boiling water to just cover, then cover with clingfilm and leave to stand for 6–8 minutes or until the water is absorbed. Meanwhile, put 300 g (10 oz) drained and chopped roasted mixed peppers from a jar, 1 finely chopped red onion and a large handful each of chopped mint and coriander leaves in a large salad bowl. Mix together 2 teaspoons harissa paste, 4 tablespoons extra-virgin olive oil and the juice of 1 lemon in a small bowl, then season. Gently fork the couscous to separate the grains and add to the salad bowl. Stir the dressing into the couscous mixture, toss to mix well and serve.

 Moroccan Kebabs

Cut 2 large courgettes, 2 cored and deseeded red peppers and 1 aubergine into chunks and put in a large bowl. Mix together 8 tablespoons olive oil, 1 tablespoon harissa paste, the juice of 2 lemons and a small handful of chopped coriander, pour over the vegetables and toss. Thread the veg on to 12 metal skewers, season and cook under a preheated medium grill for 10–12 minutes, turning once. Serve with couscous.

1. Cumin Potatoes with Pomegranate Seeds

Serves 4

½ large pomegranate
4 tablespoons sunflower oil
1–2 teaspoons black mustard seeds
1 teaspoon hot chilli powder
4 teaspoons cumin seeds
2 teaspoons sesame seeds
8–10 fresh curry leaves (optional)
2 teaspoons ground cumin
2 teaspoons ground coriander
1 teaspoon ground turmeric
500 g (1 lb) cooked potatoes, cut into 2.5 cm (1 inch) cubes
6 tablespoons chopped coriander leaves
juice of 1 small lemon
salt and pepper

· To remove the pomegranate seeds, place the pomegranate over a bowl, cut-side down, and hit with the back of a spoon, catching the seeds in the bowl. Set aside.

· Heat the oil in a large wok or frying pan until hot, add the mustard seeds and cook over a medium-high heat for a few minutes until the seeds begin to pop, then add the chilli powder, cumin seeds, sesame seeds and curry leaves, if using, and stir-fry for 30 seconds until fragrant.

· Add the ground spices and potatoes and season well, then increase the heat to high and stir-fry briskly for 4–5 minutes.

· Remove from the heat and stir in the chopped coriander and pomegranate seeds. Stir in the lemon juice, then spoon into a warm serving dish and serve hot.

2. Cumin Potato Curry

Heat 1 tablespoon sunflower oil in a heavy-based saucepan, add 1 chopped onion and cook over a high heat, stirring, for 1–2 minutes. Add 2 teaspoons cumin seeds, 1 teaspoon black mustard seeds, 2 teaspoons ground coriander, 1 teaspoon ground cumin, 1 teaspoon ground turmeric, 1 teaspoon ginger paste and 1 teaspoon garlic paste and cook for a further 1–2 minutes. Add 800 g (1¾ lb) peeled potatoes, cut into 1 cm (½ inch) cubes, 4 ripe chopped tomatoes and 300 ml (½ pint) hot vegetable stock and bring to the boil. Season, then reduce the heat to medium and simmer for 12–15 minutes or until the potatoes are tender. Remove from the heat and stir in a small handful of chopped coriander leaves. Serve with steamed rice or crusty bread.

3. Roast Cumin Potato Wedges

Cut 1 kg (2¼ lb) large baking potatoes into wedges and cook in a saucepan of boiling water for 6–8 minutes. Drain well, then place in a large bowl. Mix together 3 teaspoons cumin seeds, 1 teaspoon black mustard seeds, 2 teaspoons crushed coriander seeds, 1 tablespoon hot curry powder and 6 tablespoons sunflower oil, season with sea salt, then drizzle over the potatoes. Toss to mix well. Spread the potatoes in a single layer on a nonstick baking sheet and place in a preheated oven, 220°C (425°F), Gas Mark 7, for 20–25 minutes.

10 Spiced Red Cabbage and Carrot Salad

Serves 4

3 large carrots, peeled
½ small red cabbage, about
  250–300 g (8–10 oz)
juice of 2 lemons
1 tablespoon caster sugar
1 tablespoon light olive oil
1 teaspoon nigella seeds (black
  onion seeds)
1 teaspoon crushed coriander
  seeds
1 green chilli, deseeded and
  finely chopped
salt

- Coarsely grate the carrots, or thinly shred using a mandolin, and put in a large salad bowl. Finely slice the red cabbage into thin shreds, add to the carrots and toss together.

- Whisk together the remaining ingredients in a small bowl, then season with salt. Pour the dressing over the vegetables, toss to mix well and serve at room temperature.

---

20 Spicy Cabbage and Carrot Stir-Fry

Heat 2 tablespoons sunflower oil in a large wok, add 2 sliced red onions and cook over a medium-low heat, stirring occasionally, for 6–8 minutes until softened. Increase the heat to high, stir in 2 chopped garlic cloves, 1 deseeded and sliced green chilli, 1 teaspoon cumin seeds and 1 teaspoon medium or hot curry powder and stir-fry for 1–2 minutes, then add 300 g (10 oz) finely shredded red cabbage and 2 peeled and coarsely grated carrots and stir-fry for a further 6–8 minutes or until tender. Season, then serve with poppadums and yogurt.

30 Spicy Cabbage and Carrot Casserole

Cut 1 large red cabbage into 8 wedges and place in a deep casserole dish with 4 peeled and roughly chopped carrots. Mix together 2 tablespoons sunflower oil, 2 finely chopped garlic cloves, 1 teaspoon peeled and grated fresh root ginger, 1 deseeded and finely diced green chilli, 1 tablespoon medium or hot curry powder and 3 tablespoons sherry vinegar in a small bowl, then season. Pour the mixture over the vegetables and toss to coat evenly. Cover the casserole dish with the lid and place in a preheated oven,

200°C (400°F), Gas Mark 6, for 20–25 minutes or until tender. Serve immediately with brown rice or crusty bread.

HOT-VEGE-BAH

30 Spiced Carrot and Green Bean Stew

Serves 4

1 tablespoon sunflower oil

1 onion, sliced

1–2 hot green chillies, deseeded and sliced

1 garlic clove, crushed

5–6 fresh curry leaves

1 tablespoon medium curry powder

¼ teaspoon ground turmeric

½ teaspoon fenugreek seeds

2 carrots, peeled and cut into thin matchsticks

450 g (14½ oz) green beans, trimmed and halved

400 ml (14 fl oz) can coconut milk

juice of 1 lime

salt and pepper

steamed rice or bread, to serve

- Heat the oil in a heavy-based saucepan, add the onion, chillies, garlic and curry leaves and cook over a medium heat, stirring occasionally, for 6–8 minutes until the onion is softened and golden brown. Sprinkle over the curry powder, turmeric and fenugreek seeds and season well.

- Add the carrots and beans and cook, stirring, for a further 3–4 minutes. Reduce the heat to low, pour over the coconut milk and simmer for 10–12 minutes or until the vegetables are tender.

- Remove from the heat and stir in the lime juice. Ladle into warm bowls and serve with steamed rice or bread, if liked.

 Spiced Carrot and Green Bean Slaw

Cook 300 g (10 oz) trimmed and halved green beans in a saucepan of salted boiling water for 2–3 minutes until just tender. Drain and put in a salad bowl with 3 peeled and coarsely grated carrots. Heat 4 tablespoons olive oil in a frying pan, add 2 teaspoons black mustard seeds, 2 teaspoons cumin seeds, 1 deseeded and chopped red chilli, 1 teaspoon coriander seeds and 6–8 fresh curry leaves. Cook over a medium heat until the mustard seeds start to pop, then pour the oil mixture over the vegetables. Season and toss to mix well.

 Spicy Carrot and Green Bean Soup

Heat 1 tablespoon butter and 1 tablespoon sunflower oil in a heavy-based saucepan, add 1 finely chopped onion, 1 chopped garlic clove, 1 teaspoon peeled and grated fresh root ginger and 1 tablespoon mild curry powder and fry, stirring, for 1–2 minutes. Stir in 3 peeled and finely chopped carrots, 200 g (7 oz) finely chopped trimmed green beans and 800 ml (1 pint 8 fl oz) hot vegetable stock and bring to the boil, then reduce the heat to medium and cook for 12–15 minutes or until the vegetables are tender. Remove from the heat and, using an electric stick blender, process the soup until smooth. Season, then stir in 200 ml (7 fl oz) single cream. Serve with crusty bread.

30 Spicy Mushroom, Cauliflower and Chickpea Stew

Serves 4

2 tablespoons sunflower oil

8 spring onions, cut into 5 cm (2 inch) lengths

2 teaspoons grated garlic

2 teaspoons ground ginger

2 tablespoons hot curry powder

200 g (7 oz) baby button mushrooms

300 g (10 oz) cauliflower florets

2 red peppers, halved lengthways, deseeded and cut into chunks

400 g (13 oz) can chopped tomatoes

220 g (7½ oz) can chickpeas, rinsed and drained

3–4 tablespoons natural yogurt

salt and pepper

large handful of chopped mint leaves, to garnish

warm naan bread or steamed rice, to serve

- Heat the oil in a large frying pan, add the spring onions and fry over a medium heat for 1–2 minutes. Add the garlic, ground ginger and curry powder and fry, stirring, for 20–30 seconds until fragrant, then stir in the mushrooms, cauliflower and red peppers and fry for a further 2–3 minutes.

- Stir in the tomatoes and bring to the boil. Cover, then reduce the heat to medium and simmer, uncovered, for 10–15 minutes, stirring occasionally. Add the chickpeas, season and bring back to the boil.

- Spoon into warm bowls, drizzle with the yogurt and scatter with chopped mint. Serve with warm naan bread or steamed rice.

---

10 Spicy Mushroom and Chickpea Soup

Heat 1 tablespoon butter in a saucepan, add 2 sliced spring onions and 1 tablespoon mild curry powder and fry, stirring, for 30 seconds. Add 2 x 400 g (13 oz) cans cream of mushroom soup and a rinsed and drained 220 g (7½ oz) can chickpeas and bring to the boil, then reduce the heat to medium and cook for a few minutes or until piping hot. Serve with warm crusty bread.

20 Spicy Mushroom, Cauliflower and Chickpea Rice Heat 2 tablespoons sunflower oil in a large wok or frying pan until hot, add 1 chopped onion, 1 deseeded and chopped red chilli, 100 g (3½ oz) button mushrooms, 1 tablespoon curry powder, 100 g (3½ oz) small cauliflower florets, 100 g (3½ oz) canned chickpeas, rinsed and drained, 1 teaspoon ginger paste and 1 teaspoon garlic paste and stir-fry over

a high heat for 6–8 minutes. Add 500 g (1 lb) shop-bought ready-cooked basmati or long-grain rice and stir-fry for a further 3–4 minutes or until piping hot. Season, then serve immediately.

30 Spinach, Tomato and Paneer Curry

Serves 4

500 g (1 lb) spinach leaves
3 tablespoons unsalted butter
2 teaspoons cumin seeds
1 red chilli, deseeded and
   finely chopped
1 onion, very finely chopped
2 plum tomatoes, finely chopped
2 teaspoons finely grated garlic
1 tablespoon peeled and finely
   grated fresh root ginger
1 teaspoon chilli powder
1 teaspoon ground coriander
250 g (8 oz) paneer (Indian
   cottage cheese), cut into
   bite-sized pieces
2 tablespoons double cream
1 teaspoon lemon juice
2 tablespoons finely chopped
   coriander leaves
salt and pepper
flatbreads, to serve (optional)

- Cook the spinach in a large saucepan of boiling water for 2–3 minutes, then drain well. Transfer to a food processor or blender and blend to a smooth purée.

- Heat the butter in a large wok or frying pan, add the cumin seeds, red chilli and onion and stir-fry over a medium-low heat for 6–8 minutes until the onions have softened. Add the tomatoes, garlic, ginger, chilli powder and ground coriander and season well. Stir through and cook for 2–3 minutes.

- Increase the heat to high, add the paneer and stir-fry for 1–2 minutes, then add the spinach purée and stir-fry for a further 4–5 minutes until well mixed and heated through.

- Remove from the heat and stir in the cream, lemon juice and chopped coriander. Spoon into warm bowls and serve with warm flatbreads, if liked.

 Spicy Spinach, Tomato and Cottage Cheese Salad Put 80 g (3 oz) baby spinach leaves and 400 g (13 oz) halved cherry tomatoes in a salad bowl. Mix together 400 g (13 oz) natural cottage cheese, 1 teaspoon ginger paste, 1 teaspoon garlic paste, 1 teaspoon chilli paste and 2 teaspoons toasted cumin seeds in a bowl, then season. Add to the spinach and tomatoes, toss gently to mix and serve with crusty bread or warm baguettes.

Spicy Spinach and Tomato Soup with Crème Fraîche Heat 1 tablespoon butter and 1 tablespoon olive oil in a large heavy-based saucepan, add 1 chopped red onion, 3 chopped garlic cloves, 1 teaspoon peeled and grated fresh root ginger, 1 deseeded and sliced red chilli, 2 teaspoons cumin seeds and 2 teaspoons mild curry powder and cook, stirring, for 2–3 minutes. Stir in 6 chopped plum tomatoes and 700 ml (1 pint 3 fl oz) hot vegetable stock and bring to the boil, then cook, uncovered, over a high heat for 6–8 minutes. Add 100 g (3½ oz) chopped spinach leaves and bring back to the boil. Remove from the heat and, using an electric stick blender, process until smooth. Season, ladle into bowls and serve with dollops of crème fraîche.

HOT-VEGE-WUZ

30 Carrot, Pea and Potato Curry

Serves 4

2 teaspoons vegetable oil

3 whole cloves

2 cinnamon sticks

2 teaspoons white poppy seeds

2 teaspoons black peppercorns

4 dried red chillies

75 g (3 oz) unsweetened desiccated coconut, lightly toasted

4 garlic cloves, roughly chopped

2 onions, roughly chopped

4 teaspoons sunflower oil

2 potatoes, peeled and chopped into 2.5 cm (1 inch) cubes

2 large carrots, peeled and chopped into 2.5 cm (1 inch) cubes

400 g (13 oz) can chopped tomatoes

200 g (7 oz) frozen peas

salt

mini naan breads, to serve

- To make the spice paste, heat the vegetable oil in a small frying pan over a medium heat, add the cloves, cinnamon sticks, poppy seeds, peppercorns and dried chillies and fry for 1–2 minutes until fragrant. Put in a food processor or blender with the coconut, garlic and onions and blitz to a coarse paste.

- Heat the sunflower oil in a heavy-based saucepan, add the potatoes and carrots, then cover and cook over a medium heat for 2 minutes. Stir in the spice paste and chopped tomatoes and season with salt.

- Stir, re-cover and simmer for 15–20 minutes or until the potatoes and carrots are tender, adding the peas 5 minutes before the end of the cooking time.

- Spoon into warm bowls and serve with mini naan breads.

 Spicy Pea, Carrot and Potato Stir-Fry

Heat 2 tablespoons olive oil in a large wok until hot, add 2 teaspoons black mustard seeds and cook over a high heat until the seeds begin to pop. Add 2 teaspoons cumin seeds, 1 teaspoon ground cumin, 1 teaspoon ground coriander, 2 teaspoons hot chilli powder, a drained 300 g (10 oz) can new potatoes, diced, a drained 300 g (10 oz) can baby carrots, diced and 300 g (10 oz) frozen peas. Stir-fry over a high heat for 4–5 minutes. Remove from the heat, squeeze over the juice of 1 lemon and serve.

 Spicy Pea, Carrot and Potato Frittata

Heat 2 tablespoons sunflower oil in a medium ovenproof frying pan, add 1 chopped onion, 2 teaspoons cumin seeds, 1 tablespoon hot curry powder, a drained 300 g (10 oz) can new potatoes, diced, 200 g (7 oz) drained canned baby carrots in water, diced and 200 g (7 oz) fresh or frozen peas and cook over a high heat, stirring, for 3–4 minutes. Lightly beat 6 eggs in a bowl, then season and pour into the pan. Cook for 8–10 minutes or until the base is set, then place the pan under a preheated medium-hot grill and cook for 3–4 minutes or until the top is golden and set. Serve immediately with a crisp green salad.

Chinese-Style Runner Beans with Chilli

Serves 4

600 g (1 lb 5 oz) stringless runner beans, trimmed and cut into 2 cm (¾ inch) pieces
3 tablespoons sunflower oil
1 teaspoon ground turmeric
salt
egg-fried rice, to serve (optional)

For the chilli paste

2 red chillies, deseeded and roughly chopped
4 shallots, roughly chopped
2 garlic cloves, finely chopped
2 teaspoons peeled and grated fresh root ginger
4 tablespoons light soy sauce

• Cook the beans in a large saucepan of lightly salted boiling water for 3–4 minutes or until tender. Drain well, then set aside.

• To make the chilli paste, put all the ingredients in a food processor or blender and blend to a smooth paste, adding a little water to loosen the mixture if needed.

• Heat the oil in a large wok or frying pan until hot, stir in the chilli paste and stir-fry over a medium heat for 2–3 minutes until fragrant. Add the drained beans and the turmeric, season with salt and stir-fry for a further 2–3 minutes or until piping hot. Serve immediately with egg-fried rice, if liked.

---

1 Runner Bean, Chilli and Egg-Fried Rice

Heat 2 tablespoons sunflower oil in a large wok or frying pan until hot, add 300 g (10 oz) finely sliced runner beans and stir-fry over a high heat for 1–2 minutes. Add a 500 g (1 lb) tub fresh egg-fried rice, 1 tablespoon hot chilli sauce, 2 tablespoons sweet chilli sauce and 2 tablespoons light soy sauce and stir-fry for a further 3–4 minutes or until piping hot. Serve immediately.

3 Spiced Runner Bean and Chilli Pilau

Heat 2 tablespoons sunflower oil in a heavy-based saucepan, add 6 chopped shallots and cook over a medium heat for 3–4 minutes, stirring occasionally, until softened. Stir in 2 teaspoons cumin seeds, 1 cinnamon stick, 1 bay leaf, 6 green cardamom pods, 10 peppercorns, 4 cloves and 4 dried red chillies and cook, stirring, for a further 1–2 minutes. Add 400 g (13 oz) basmati rice and 400 g (13 oz) sliced runner beans and stir until well coated, then pour in 800 ml (1 pint 8 fl oz) hot vegetable stock and bring to the boil. Cover tightly, reduce the heat to low and cook, undisturbed, for 15–20 minutes or until the liquid is absorbed and the rice is tender. Remove from the heat and leave to stand for a few minutes before serving with pickles and poppadums.

Curried Mushrooms and Tomatoes

Serves 4

5 tablespoons sunflower oil
500 g (1 lb) chestnut mushrooms, halved or thickly sliced
100 ml (3½ fl oz) double cream
2 ripe plum tomatoes, finely chopped
6 tablespoons finely chopped coriander leaves
salt and pepper
steamed rice, to serve

For the spice paste

4 garlic cloves, finely chopped
2 teaspoons peeled and finely chopped fresh root ginger
1 onion, finely chopped
1 tablespoon medium or hot curry powder
3 tablespoons water

- To make the spice paste, put all the ingredients in a food processor or blender and blend until smooth.

- Heat 3 tablespoons of the oil in a large wok until hot, add the mushrooms and stir fry over a high heat for 4–5 minutes. Transfer the contents of the wok to a bowl and wipe out the wok with kitchen paper.

- Heat the remaining oil in the wok until hot, add the curry paste and stir-fry over a medium heat for 3–4 minutes. Return the mushrooms and any juices to the wok, add the cream and tomato and cook, stirring, for 3–4 minutes or until piping hot. Season well.

- Remove from the heat, stir in the chopped coriander and serve immediately with steamed rice.

 Spicy Mushroom and Tomato Stir-Fry

Heat 2 tablespoons sunflower oil in a large wok or frying pan until hot, add 500 g (1 lb) large sliced chestnut mushrooms, 1 tablespoon medium or hot curry powder, 1 teaspoon ginger paste and 1 teaspoon garlic paste and stir-fry over a high heat for 4–5 minutes. Stir in 100 ml (3½ fl oz) double cream and 2 chopped tomatoes and cook for 2–3 minutes or until piping hot. Scatter with a small handful of chopped coriander and serve with steamed rice or noodles.

 Spicy Mushroom and Tomato Rice

Heat 2 tablespoons sunflower oil in a heavy-based saucepan, add 1 chopped onion, 1 teaspoon garlic paste, 1 tablespoon medium or hot curry powder, 500 g (1 lb) chopped mushrooms and 2 chopped tomatoes and cook, stirring, for 1–2 minutes until softened. Add 400 g (13 oz) basmati rice and stir until well coated, then pour in 800 ml (1 pint 8 fl oz) hot vegetable stock and bring to the boil. Season, then cover tightly, reduce the heat to low and cook, undisturbed, for 15–20 minutes or until the liquid is absorbed and the rice is tender. Remove from the heat and leave to stand for a few minutes before serving.

HOT-VEGE-RES

 # Indonesian Okra with Coconut

Serves 4

2 tablespoons sunflower oil

1 onion, finely chopped

1 tablespoon black mustard seeds

1 tablespoon cumin seeds

2–3 dried red chillies

10–12 fresh curry leaves

600 g (1 lb 5 oz) okra, cut
   diagonally into 1.5 cm
   (¾ inch) lengths

1 teaspoon ground turmeric

100 g (3½ oz) grated fresh
   coconut

salt and pepper

steamed rice, to serve (optional)

- Heat the oil in a large wok or frying pan until hot, add the onion and stir-fry over a medium heat for 5–6 minutes until softened.

- Increase the heat to medium-high, add the mustard seeds and stir-fry for a few minutes until the seeds begin to pop, then add the cumin seeds, dried chillies and curry leaves and stir-fry for a further 2 minutes until fragrant.

- Stir in the okra and turmeric and continue to stir-fry for 3–4 minutes, then season well.

- Spoon on to warm serving plates and sprinkle over the coconut. Serve immediately with steamed rice, if liked.

 Spicy Coconut Soup with Deep-Fried Okra Put 600 ml (1 pint) hot vegetable stock, a 400 ml (14 fl oz) can coconut milk and 1 tablespoon mild curry paste in a large saucepan and bring to the boil, then reduce the heat to medium, season and cook for 4–5 minutes. Meanwhile, fill a wok or small, deep saucepan one-quarter full with sunflower oil and heat to 180°C–190°C (350°F–375°F), or until a cube of bread browns in 30 seconds. Deep-fry 8 finely sliced okra in the oil for 1 minute until crispy. Remove with a slotted spoon and drain on kitchen paper. To serve, ladle the soup into warm bowls and sprinkle over the fried okra.

Spiced Coconut and Okra Rice Heat 2 tablespoons sunflower oil in a heavy-based saucepan, add 1 tablespoon black mustard seeds and cook over a medium-high heat for a few minutes until the seeds begin to pop, then add 1 finely chopped onion, 2 teaspoons cumin seeds, 2 dried red chillies and 10 fresh curry leaves and cook, stirring, for 3–4 minutes until the onion is softened. Add 400 g (13 oz) basmati rice and stir until the grains are well coated. Add 300 g (10 oz) thickly sliced okra, then pour in a 400 ml (14 fl oz) can coconut milk and 400 ml (14 fl oz) hot vegetable stock. Bring to the boil, then cover tightly, reduce the heat to low and cook, undisturbed, for 15–20 minutes or until the liquid is absorbed and the rice is tender. Remove from the heat and leave to stand for a few minutes before serving.

30 Butternut Squash and Red Pepper Curry

Serves 4

2 tablespoons sunflower oil
1 red onion, thinly sliced
2 garlic cloves, minced
1 teaspoon peeled and finely
    grated fresh root ginger
3 tablespoons Thai red curry paste
800 g (1¾ lb) butternut squash,
    peeled, deseeded and cut into
    bite-sized cubes
2 red peppers, cored, deseeded
    and cut into bite-sized pieces
400 ml (14 fl oz) can coconut milk
200 ml (7 fl oz) water
6 kaffir lime leaves
2 teaspoons grated palm sugar
    or caster sugar
3 lemon grass stalks, bruised
50 g (2 oz) skinless raw peanuts
small handful of Thai basil leaves
salt and pepper
steamed jasmine rice, to serve

- Heat the oil in a large wok or frying pan until hot, add the onion, garlic and ginger and stir-fry over a medium heat for 1–2 minutes until softened. Stir in the curry paste, butternut squash and red peppers and stir-fry for a further 2–3 minutes.

- Pour over the coconut milk and measurement water and add the lime leaves, sugar and lemon grass. Bring to the boil, then reduce the heat to low and simmer gently, uncovered, stirring occasionally, for 15–20 minutes or until the squash is tender. Season to taste.

- Meanwhile, heat a small nonstick frying pan until hot, add the peanuts and dry-fry for 3–4 minutes or until toasted. Leave to cool, then roughly chop.

- Ladle the curry into warm bowls, scatter over the Thai basil leaves and chopped peanuts and serve with steamed jasmine rice.

---

10 Curried Butternut Squash and Red Pepper Soup Heat 1 tablespoon sunflower oil in a saucepan, add 1 tablespoon mild curry paste and 1 teaspoon lemon grass paste and stir for 30–40 seconds. Add 2 x 400 g (13 oz) cans root vegetable and butternut squash soup and 1 cored, deseeded and finely diced red pepper and bring to the boil. Reduce the heat to medium and cook for 4–5 minutes or until piping hot. Serve with warm bread rolls.

20 Curried Roast Butternut Squash and Red Peppers Put 600 g (1 lb 5 oz) peeled and deseeded butternut squash, cut into 1.5 cm (¾ inch) cubes, and 2 cored and deseeded red peppers, cut into bite-sized pieces, in a roasting tin. Mix together 6 tablespoons sunflower oil, 1 tablespoon medium curry paste, 1 teaspoon lemon grass paste and 200 ml (7 fl oz) coconut cream in a bowl. Pour the mixture over the vegetables, season and toss to mix well. Place in a preheated oven, 220°C (425°F), Gas Mark 7, for 15 minutes or until tender. Serve with rice or warm flatbreads.

30 Middle Eastern Courgette, Tomato and Mint Curry

Serves 4

2 tablespoons olive oil

2 onions, finely sliced

4 courgettes, cut into 1 cm
(½ inch) cubes

2 x 400 g (13 oz) cans peeled
plum tomatoes

2 garlic cloves, crushed

1 teaspoon mild chilli powder

¼ teaspoon ground turmeric

2 teaspoons dried mint

salt and pepper

small handful of finely chopped
mint leaves, to garnish

· Heat the oil in a large heavy-based saucepan, add the onion and cook over a medium-low heat, stirring occasionally, for 6-8 minutes until softened. Add the courgettes and cook, stirring occasionally, for a further 5-6 minutes until tender.

· Increase the heat to medium, add the tomatoes and garlic and cook for 10–12 minutes until the sauce is thickened. Stir in the chilli powder, turmeric and mint and cook for a further 2–3 minutes. Season well.

· Ladle into warm bowls and serve scattered with the chopped mint leaves.

 Spicy Courgette, Tomato and Mint Salad Coarsely grate 2 large courgettes and put in a salad bowl with 6 finely chopped tomatoes and a large handful of mint leaves. Mix together 6 tablespoons extra-virgin olive oil, 1 teaspoon mild chilli powder, 1 teaspoon garlic paste, 2 teaspoons runny honey and the juice of 2 lemons in a bowl, then season. Pour the dressing over the salad, toss to mix well and serve.

20 Griddled Spicy Courgettes with Tomato and Mint Thinly slice 3 large courgettes lengthways. Brush the slices with olive oil and sprinkle over 2 teaspoons mild curry powder. Toss to mix well, then cook in batches on a preheated hot griddle pan for 2–3 minutes on each side. Transfer to a serving plate in a single layer. Scatter over 4 finely diced plum tomatoes and a large handful of torn mint leaves. Squeeze over the juice of 2 lemons, drizzle over 3 table-spoons extra-virgin olive oil, season and serve with warm pitta breads.

Deep-Fried Spiced Baby Aubergine

Serves 4

600 g baby aubergines
2 tablespoons curry powder
sunflower oil, for deep-frying
small handful of chopped mint
  leaves, to garnish
salt

To serve

lemon wedges
chilli powder
sea salt

- Thinly slice the aubergines and place in a bowl with the curry powder. Season with salt and toss to mix well.

  Fill a wok or small, deep saucepan one-quarter full with sunflower oil and heat to 180°C–190°C (350°F–375°F), or until a cube of bread browns in 30 seconds. Deep-fry the aubergines, in 2 or 3 batches, for 1–2 minutes or until crisp and golden. Drain on kitchen paper.

- Transfer the aubergines to a large serving plate, scatter over a small handful of chopped mint and serve immediately with lemon wedges and a sprinkling of chilli powder and sea salt.

 ### Spicy Aubergine Pilaff

Heat 2 tablespoons sunflower oil in a heavy-based saucepan, add 1 finely chopped onion and cook over a medium heat for 4–5 minutes. Stir in 2 teaspoons cumin seeds and 1 teaspoon black mustard seeds and cook for 40–50 seconds. Add 275 g (9 oz) basmati rice, stir until well coated and season well. Add 600 ml (1 pint) hot vegetable stock and bring to the boil. Cover, reduce the heat to low and cook for 12–15 minutes or until the liquid is absorbed. Meanwhile, cut 600 g (1 lb 5 oz) baby aubergines into 1 cm (½ inch) cubes. Heat 2 tablespoons oil in a large frying pan, add the aubergines and fry for 6–8 minutes or until tender and cooked through. Stir in 1 tablespoon medium or hot curry powder and cook for a further 1–2 minutes, then season. Stir the aubergines into the cooked rice with a handful of chopped mint leaves. Serve with dollops of yogurt.

 ### Spiced Baby Chilli Aubergines

Blend 2 chopped red chillies, 1 tablespoon peeled and finely grated root ginger, 4 grated garlic cloves and 400 g (7 oz) chopped tomatoes until smooth. Heat 250 ml (8 fl oz) sunflower oil in a frying pan. Add 750 g baby aubergine halves and cook for 2–3 minutes. Remove to kitchen paper. In the pan, stir-fry 2 teaspoons each fennel and nigella seeds for 1 minute. Stir in the puréed mixture, 1 tablespoon ground coriander, 1 teaspoon paprika and ¼ teaspoon ground turmeric, season and simmer over medium heat for 5 minutes, stirring, until the mixture thickens. Return the aubergine to the pan, toss to coat, cover and cook for 10 minutes. Stir in a handful of chopped coriander and mint. Serve.

HOT-VEGE-BAB

Spiced Okra, Tomato and Coconut

Serves 4

2 tablespoons sunflower oil
6–8 fresh curry leaves
2 teaspoons black mustard seeds
1 onion, finely chopped
2 teaspoons ground cumin
1 teaspoon ground coriander
2 teaspoons medium or hot
  curry powder
1 teaspoon ground turmeric
3 garlic cloves, finely chopped
500 g (1 lb) okra, trimmed and cut
  diagonally into 2.5 cm (1 in) pieces
2 ripe plum tomatoes, chopped
3 tablespoons grated fresh
  coconut, to garnish
salt and pepper

- Heat the oil in a large wok or frying pan until hot, add the curry leaves, mustard seeds and onion and stir-fry over a medium heat for 3–4 minutes until fragrant and the onion is beginning to soften. Add the cumin, ground coriander, curry powder and turmeric and stir-fry for a further 30 seconds until fragrant.

- Add the garlic and okra, increase the heat to high and stir-fry for 2–3 minutes, then add the tomatoes and season well. Cover, then reduce the heat to low and cook gently, stirring occasionally, for 10–12 minutes or until the okra is just tender.

- Remove from the heat and sprinkle over the coconut, then ladle into warm bowls and serve.

Spicy Fried Okra with Coconut

Fill a wok one-quarter full with sunflower oil and heat to 180°C–190°C (350°F–375°F), or until a cube of bread browns in 30 seconds. Put 500 g (1 lb) sliced okra in a bowl with 2 teaspoons cornflour, 2 teaspoons each ground cumin and hot chilli powder and 1 teaspoon ground coriander and toss to mix. Deep-fry the okra in batches for 1–2 minutes until crisp. Remove from the oil using a slotted spoon and drain on kitchen paper. Sprinkle over 4 tablespoons grated fresh coconut and season with salt. Serve with rice and natural yogurt.

Tomato, Coconut and Okra Curry

Heat 2 tablespoons sunflower oil in a large saucepan, add 1 chopped onion and cook over a medium heat, stirring occasionally, for 4–5 minutes until softened. Stir in a 400 g (13 oz) can chopped tomatoes and 2 tablespoons medium or hot curry powder, increase the heat to high and cook for 4–5 minutes, then add a 400 ml (14 fl oz) can coconut milk and bring back to the boil. Add 500 g (1 lb) okra, trimmed and cut into 2 cm (¾ inch) pieces, then reduce the heat to medium, cover and simmer gently for 10–12 minutes or until the okra is just tender. Season well. Serve with steamed rice and warm naan breads.

Spicy Tofu with Pak Choi and Spring Onions

Serves 4

2 tablespoons sunflower oil
2 teaspoons grated fresh root ginger
8 garlic cloves, roughly chopped
4 shallots, finely chopped
2 red chillies, deseeded and chopped
8 cm (3 inch) length of trimmed
  lemon grass stalk, finely chopped
1 teaspoon ground turmeric
400 ml (14 fl oz) can coconut milk
200 ml (7 fl oz) hot vegetable stock
400 g (13 oz) baby pak choi,
  halved or quartered
200 g (7 oz) mangetout
400 g (14 oz) firm tofu, cubed
1 tablespoon dark soy sauce
1 tablespoon lime juice
6 spring onions, thinly sliced
salt and pepper

To garnish

small handful of Thai basil leaves
sliced red chillies

Put the oil, ginger, garlic, shallots, chopped red chillies, lemon grass, turmeric and half the coconut milk in a food processor or blender and blend until fairly smooth.

- Heat a large nonstick wok or frying pan until hot, add the coconut milk mixture and stir-fry over a high heat for 3–4 minutes. Add the remaining coconut milk and the stock and bring to the boil, then reduce the heat to low and simmer gently, uncovered, for 6–8 minutes.

- Add the pak choi, mangetout and tofu and simmer for a further 6–7 minutes. Stir in the soy sauce and lime juice, then season to taste and simmer for another 1–2 minutes.

- Remove from the heat and stir in the spring onions. Ladle into warm bowls and serve scattered with Thai basil leaves and sliced red chillies.

 Japanese-Style Tofu with Spring Onions
Cut 800 g (1¾ lb) firm tofu into cubes and place in a dish. Mix together 1 tablespoon sesame oil, 2 tablespoons sunflower oil, 1 tablespoon mirin, 4 tablespoons light soy sauce, 1 deseeded and diced red chilli and 1 teaspoon chilli powder mixed with 1 teaspoon sesame seeds and drizzle over the tofu. Sprinkle over 8 finely sliced spring onions and serve.

 Spicy Tofu and Spring Onion Stir-Fry Heat 2 tablespoons sunflower oil in a wok or frying pan until hot, add 3 crushed garlic cloves and 1 teaspoon peeled and grated fresh root ginger and stir-fry over a high heat for 10–20 seconds. Stir in 12 thickly sliced spring onions, 600 g (1 lb 5 oz) cubed firm tofu and 1 deseeded and diced red chilli and stir-fry for a further 4–5 minutes or until the tofu is lightly browned. Add 100 ml (3½ fl oz) hot vegetable stock and 2 tablespoons dark soy sauce, reduce the heat to medium and cook for 6–8 minutes or until all the liquid is absorbed. Stir in a 300 g (10 oz) bag fresh egg noodles and cook for a further 3–4 minutes. Serve immediately.

Malaysian Red Pepper and Cabbage Stir-Fry

Serves 4

1 tablespoon sunflower oil

2 garlic cloves, crushed

2 teaspoons medium curry powder

1 red pepper, cored, deseeded and finely diced

½ green cabbage, finely shredded

3 eggs, lightly beaten

salt and pepper

crusty bread, to serve (optional)

- Heat the oil in a large wok or frying pan until hot, add the garlic, curry powder and red pepper and stir-fry over a medium-high heat for 3–4 minutes until softened.

- Increase the heat to high, add the cabbage, season and stir-fry for 5 minutes or until the cabbage is cooked but still retains a bite.

- Stir in the eggs and mix well with the vegetables, then continue stirring until the eggs are scrambled and just cooked through. Serve immediately with crusty bread, if liked.

 Spicy Cabbage and Red Pepper Salad

Put ½ green cabbage, finely shredded, and 200 g (7 oz) roasted red peppers from a jar, sliced, in a large salad bowl. Mix together 150 ml (¼ pint) shop-bought French salad dressing, 1 teaspoon garlic paste and ½ teaspoon mild curry powder in a small bowl, then season. Pour the dressing over the salad, toss to mix well and serve.

 Spicy Cabbage and Red Pepper Stew

Heat 2 tablespoons sunflower oil in a large saucepan, add 2 finely sliced onions and cook over a medium heat, stirring occasionally, for 6–8 minutes or until soft and translucent. Stir in 3 chopped garlic cloves, 1 deseeded and sliced red chilli and 1 tablespoon mild curry paste, then pour over 400 ml (14 fl oz) hot vegetable stock and a 400 ml (14 fl oz) can coconut milk and bring to the boil. Stir in ½ green cabbage, shredded, and 3 cored, deseeded and thinly sliced red peppers and bring back to the boil, then reduce the heat to medium and cook for 12–15 minutes or until the vegetables are tender. Season well, then serve with rice or crusty bread.

HOT-VEGE-CYF

30 Spanish Potatoes with Spicy Tomatoes

Serves 4

800 g (1¾ lb) potatoes, peeled
and cut into small cubes
2 tablespoons olive oil
400 g (13 oz) can chopped
tomatoes
1 small red onion, finely chopped
2 garlic cloves, finely chopped
1 teaspoon dried red chilli flakes
1 teaspoon cayenne pepper
3 teaspoons sweet
smoked paprika
1 bay leaf
1 teaspoon golden caster sugar
salt and pepper
finely chopped flat leaf parsley,
to garnish
crusty bread, to serve

- Cook the potatoes in a large saucepan of salted boiling water for 10–12 minutes or until tender, then drain well.

- Line a baking sheet with nonstick baking paper. Place the potatoes in a single layer on the sheet, drizzle over the oil and season. Place in a preheated oven, 220°C (425°F), Gas Mark 7, for 10–12 minutes or until lightly browned.

- Meanwhile, put the tomatoes, red onion, garlic, chilli flakes and cayenne pepper in a saucepan and cook over a medium heat for 10 minutes, stirring occasionally then stir in the paprika, bay leaf and sugar and cook for a further 4–5 minutes until thickened.

- Transfer the potatoes to a warm serving dish, then pour over the spicy tomato sauce and toss to mix well. Scatter with chopped parsley and serve with crusty bread.

---

1 Spicy Potato and Tomato Stir-Fry

Heat 2 tablespoons sunflower oil in a large wok or frying pan until hot, add a drained 540 g (1 lb 3 oz) can new potatoes, cubed, 1 roughly chopped onion, 1 teaspoon dried red chilli flakes, 1 tablespoon sweet smoked paprika and 2 diced plum tomatoes and stir-fry over a high heat for 5–6 minutes or until piping hot, then season. Serve with a green salad and warm bread.

2 Spicy Warm Potato and Tomato Salad

Cook 800 g (1¾ lb) halved Charlotte or baby new potatoes in a large saucepan of salted boiling water for 10–12 minutes or until just tender. Meanwhile, heat 6 tablespoons olive oil in a large frying pan, add 2 chopped garlic cloves, 1 roughly chopped onion, 1 teaspoon dried red chilli flakes and 1 teaspoon sweet smoked paprika and cook over a medium heat for 8–10 minutes, stirring occasionally, until the onion is softened. Drain the potatoes and put in a large serving bowl with 4 chopped plum tomatoes. Add the onion mixture with a handful of chopped flat leaf parsley. Season, toss to mix well and serve warm or at room temperature.

Thai Massaman Pumpkin Curry

Serves 4

2 tablespoons vegetable oil

2 tablespoons Thai massaman
curry paste

6 shallots, thinly sliced

8 cm (3 inch) length of trimmed
lemon grass stalk, finely chopped

6 green cardamom pods

2 teaspoons black mustard seeds

800 g (1¾ lb) pumpkin flesh,
cut into 1 cm (½ inch) cubes

200 ml (7 fl oz) hot vegetable stock

400 ml (14 fl oz) can coconut milk

juice of 1 lime

To garnish

small handful of Thai basil leaves
or mint leaves

red chilli slivers

To serve (optional)

lime wedges

steamed jasmine rice

· Heat the oil in a heavy-based saucepan, add the curry paste, shallots, lemon grass, cardamom and mustard seeds and fry over a medium heat for 1–2 minutes until fragrant.

· Add the pumpkin and pour over the stock and coconut milk. Bring to a simmer, then cook for 10–12 minutes or until the pumpkin is tender.

· Remove from the heat and stir in the lime juice. Ladle into warm bowls, scatter with Thai basil or mint leaves and red chilli slivers and serve with lime wedges for squeezing over and steamed jasmine rice, if liked.

**Thai Massaman
Vegetable Stir-Fry**

Heat 2 tablespoons sunflower oil in a large wok or frying pan until hot, add 2 x 230 g (7½ oz) packs ready-prepared hot and spicy stir-fry vegetables and 1 tablespoon massaman curry paste and stir-fry over a high heat for 1–2 minutes. Pour in 200 ml (7 fl oz) canned coconut milk and stir-fry for a further 3–4 minutes or until the vegetables are tender. Serve with rice or noodles.

**Spicy Roast
Thai Massaman
Vegetables** Cut 500 g (1 lb) peeled and deseeded pumpkin, 2 cored and deseeded red peppers and 1 large aubergine into 2 cm (¾ inch) cubes and place in an ovenproof dish. Mix together 2 tablespoons Thai massaman curry paste and 200 ml (7 fl oz) canned coconut milk in a bowl. Pour the mixture over the vegetables, toss to mix well and season with salt. Place

in a preheated oven, 200°C (400°F), Gas Mark 6, for 20–25 minutes or until tender. Scatter with a small handful of Thai basil or mint leaves and serve with steamed rice.

HOT-VEGE-CIR

QuickCook

Pulses, Pods and Grains

Recipes listed by cooking time

30

20

Warm Soya Bean, Ginger, Chilli and Noodle Salad

Serves 4

250 g (8 oz) dried soba noodles

250 g (8 oz) frozen podded soya beans

6 spring onions, thinly sliced diagonally

2 tablespoons sesame seeds

3 cm (1 inch) piece of fresh root ginger

1 red chilli, finely chopped

1 tablespoon toasted sesame oil

3 tablespoons mirin

3 tablespoons light soy sauce

1 teaspoon clear honey

salt

chopped coriander leaves, to garnish

- Cook the noodles and soya beans in a large saucepan of lightly salted boiling water for 4–5 minutes, or according to the noodle packet instructions. Drain well, then return to the pan and add the spring onions. Cover and keep warm.

- Heat a frying pan until hot, add the sesame seeds and dry-fry over a medium heat until lightly golden, then remove from the pan and set aside.

- Peel and grate the root ginger into a bowl, then stir in the remaining ingredients and mix well. Pour the dressing over the noodle mixture and toss to mix well.

- Ladle into warm bowls, scatter over the sesame seeds and chopped coriander and serve.

 Soya Bean, Ginger, Chilli and Noodle Broth Put 800 ml (1 pint 8 fl oz) hot vegetable stock, 1 teaspoon peeled and grated fresh root ginger, 1 chopped red chilli and 6 finely sliced spring onions in a saucepan and bring to the boil, then add 400 g (12 oz) shop-bought ready-cooked soba noodles and 200 g (7 oz) frozen podded soya beans. Bring back to the boil, then season and serve sprinkled with chopped coriander leaves and a drizzle of sesame oil.

Soya Bean, Ginger and Chilli Rice Heat 2 tablespoons sunflower oil in a heavy-based saucepan, add 8 sliced spring onions, 2 teaspoons peeled and chopped fresh root ginger, 2 finely chopped red chillies and cook, stirring, over a low heat for 1–2 minutes, then add 250 g (8 oz) basmati rice and cook, stirring to coat the rice, for a further 1–2 minutes. Stir in 700 ml (1 pint 2 fl oz) hot vegetable stock and 200 g (10 oz) frozen podded soya beans and bring to the boil. Cover tightly, reduce the heat to low and cook, undisturbed, for 12–15 minutes or until the liquid is absorbed and the rice and beans are tender. Remove from the heat and leave to stand for 10 minutes. When ready to serve, fluff up the rice with a fork. Serve sprinkled with 4 tablespoons toasted sesame seeds and with Japanese-style pickles, if liked.

30 Vietnamese Herby Chicken Rice with Nuoc Cham Sauce

Serves 4

350 g (11½ oz) long-grain rice, rinsed and drained

850 ml (1 pint 9 fl oz) good-quality chicken stock

400 g (13 oz) boneless, skinless chicken thighs, sliced

6 shallots, finely sliced

2 red chillies, finely sliced

2 teaspoons peeled and grated fresh root ginger

handful of chopped mint leaves

handful of chopped coriander

8 spring onions, finely sliced, to garnish

For the nuoc cham sauce

2 garlic cloves, chopped

1 red chilli, chopped

1 lime

3–4 tablespoons fish sauce

1–2 tablespoons water

- To make the nuoc cham sauce, put the garlic and red chilli in a mortar and mash with the pestle to form a paste. Squeeze the juice of the lime into the paste, then remove the pulp and add it to the mixture. Mash to a paste again, then stir in enough fish sauce and water to dilute. Set aside.

- Put the rice in a heavy-based saucepan, then stir in the stock, chicken, shallots, red chillies and ginger and bring to the boil. Cover tightly, reduce the heat to low and cook, undisturbed, for 12–15 minutes or until the liquid is absorbed, the rice is tender and the chicken is cooked through.

- Remove the pan from the heat and stir in the herbs and spring onions. Cover and leave to stand for a few minutes.

- Ladle into warm bowls and serve with the nuoc cham sauce spooned over or in a bowl on the side.

10 Vietnamese Chicken, Herb and Rice Salad

Put 500 g (1 lb) shop-bought fresh basmati rice, 400 g (12 oz) shop-bought ready-cooked chicken breasts, skin removed and shredded, 1 shredded cucumber, 1 finely chopped red chilli and a small handful each of chopped mint and coriander in a large salad bowl. Make the nuoc cham sauce as above, then spoon 2 tablespoons over the salad. Toss to mix well and serve.

20 Vietnamese Chicken, Herb and Rice Soup

Heat 1 tablespoon sunflower oil in a heavy-based saucepan, add 1 chopped onion, 2 chopped garlic cloves, 1 teaspoon peeled and grated fresh root ginger, a 2 cm (¾ inch) length of trimmed lemon grass stalk, finely chopped and 1 finely chopped red chilli and cook over a low heat, stirring occasionally, for 4–5 minutes until the onion is softened. Stir in 900 ml (1½ pints) hot chicken stock and 80 g (2 oz) basmati rice and bring to the boil, then cook, uncovered, for 10–12 minutes or until the rice is tender. Stir in 400 g (12 oz) shop-bought ready-cooked chicken breasts, skin removed and shredded, and a small handful of chopped mint leaves. Serve immediately.

20 Spicy Prawn and Vegetable Noodles

Serves 4

2 tablespoons sunflower oil
400 g (13 oz) raw peeled
  tiger prawns
6 spring onions, cut diagonally
  into 2 cm (¾ inch) lengths
2 garlic cloves, crushed
1 red chilli, finely chopped
1 teaspoon grated fresh root ginger
1 red pepper, cored, deseeded and
  finely chopped
1 carrot, peeled and cut into thin
  matchsticks
100 g (3½ oz) frozen peas
500 g (1 lb) fresh egg noodles
2 tablespoons hot chilli sauce
1 tablespoon dark soy sauce
3 tablespoons sweet chilli sauce
chopped coriander leaves, to
  garnish

- Heat the oil in a large wok or frying pan until hot, add the prawns, spring onions, garlic, red chilli and ginger and stir-fry over a high heat for 4–5 minutes or until the prawns turn pink.

- Add the red pepper, carrot and peas and stir-fry over a medium-high heat for a further 3–4 minutes. Stir in the noodles, hot chilli sauce, soy sauce and sweet chilli sauce and continue to stir-fry for 3–4 minutes or until the noodles are piping hot.

- Divide into warm bowls, scatter with chopped coriander and serve immediately.

 Spicy Prawn and Vegetable Rice

Heat 2 tablespoons sunflower oil in a large wok or frying pan until hot, add a 400 g (12 oz) pack ready-prepared stir-fry vegetables and stir-fry over a high heat for 2–3 minutes, then add a 500 g (1 lb) tub fresh egg-fried rice, 200 g (10 oz) cooked peeled prawns, 2 tablespoons hot chilli sauce and a 125 g (4 oz) sachet Chinese stir-fry sauce and stir-fry for a further 1–2 minutes or until the rice is piping hot. Serve immediately.

 Spicy Prawn and Tofu Vegetables

Heat 2 tablespoons sunflower oil in a large wok or frying pan until hot, add 2 chopped shallots, 2 sliced red chillies, 2 teaspoons grated fresh root ginger, 2 teaspoons grated garlic, 1 teaspoon crushed Szechuan peppercorns and a pinch of salt and stir-fry over a medium-high heat for 1 minute. Add 150 g (5 oz) diced firm tofu and stir-fry for a further 2 minutes, then remove to a plate. Heat another 2 tablespoons sunflower oil in the wok until hot, add 1 peeled carrot, cut into matchsticks, 2 cored and deseeded red peppers, sliced, and 200 g (7 oz) mangetout, halved lengthways, and stir-fry over a high heat for 2–4 minutes or until starting to wilt, then add 2 tablespoons sweet chilli sauce, 1 tablespoon hot chilli sauce, 4 tablespoons light soy sauce and 2 tablespoons Chinese rice wine. Return the tofu to the wok with 200 g (10 oz) cooked peeled prawns, toss to mix well and heat through until piping hot. Drizzle with 1 tablespoon sesame oil and serve with cooked noodles.

Spicy Green Bean, Potato and Pesto Linguine

Serves 4

200 g (7 oz) potatoes, peeled and cut into small cubes

200 g (7 oz) green beans, trimmed and halved

350 g (11½ oz) dried linguine

2 red chillies, finely chopped

250 g (8 oz) shop-bought fresh green pesto

salt and pepper

grated pecorino cheese, to serve

- Cook the potatoes in a large saucepan of lightly salted boiling water for 10–12 minutes or until just tender, adding the beans 4 minutes before the end of the cooking time. Drain well, then return to the pan.

- Meanwhile, cook the pasta in a separate saucepan of boiling water according to the packet instructions until al dente, then drain and add to the potatoes and beans.

- Mix together the red chillies and pesto in a bowl, then season well. Spoon into the pasta mixture and toss to mix well.

- Spoon into warm bowls and serve with grated pecorino cheese to sprinkle over.

---

10 **Spicy Green Bean and Pesto Pasta Salad** Cook 200 g (10 oz) fresh penne and 500 g (1 lb) trimmed green beans in a large saucepan of lightly salted boiling water for 2–4 minutes, or according to the pasta packet instructions, until tender. Drain, then refresh under cold running water and drain again. Put the pasta and beans in a large salad bowl and add 1 sliced red onion and 200 g (7 oz) halved cherry tomatoes. Mix together 2 finely chopped red chillies and 250 g (8 oz) shop-bought fresh green pesto in a bowl. Pour over the salad, season and toss to mix well before serving.

30 **Spicy Green Bean and Pesto Pasta Gratin** Cook 250 g (11½ oz) dried penne in a large saucepan of lightly salted boiling water according to the packet instructions until al dente, adding 400 g (12 oz) trimmed and chopped green beans 2 minutes before the end of the cooking time. Meanwhile, mix together 2 finely chopped red chillies, 250 g (8 oz) shop-bought fresh green pesto, 200 g (7 oz) mascarpone cheese and 2 lightly beaten eggs. Drain the pasta and beans, then put in a lightly greased shallow ovenproof dish. Pour over the pesto mixture and toss to mix well. Sprinkle over 100 g (2½ oz) dried breadcrumbs and place in a preheated oven, 200°C (400°F), Gas Mark 6, for 10–15 minutes or until piping hot. Serve with a rocket salad.

Warm Spicy Black Bean, Spring Onion and Noodle Salad

Serves 4

250 g (8 oz) dried egg noodles
6 spring onions
2 x 400 g (13 oz) cans black
   beans, rinsed and drained
3 cm (1 inch) piece of fresh
   root ginger
2 red chillies, finely diced
1 tablespoon sesame oil
1–2 teaspoons chilli oil
3 tablespoons sweet chilli sauce
3 tablepoons light soy sauce
1 teaspoon clear honey
salt
chopped coriander leaves,
   to garnish

- Cook the noodles in a large saucepan of lightly salted boiling water for 4–5 minutes, or according to the packet instructions. Drain well, then return to the pan and cover. Thinly slice the spring onions diagonally and add to the noodles with the black beans and toss to mix well.

- Peel and grate the root ginger into a bowl, then stir in the remaining ingredients and mix well. Pour the dressing over the noodle mixture and toss to mix well. Cook over a low heat for a few minutes until warmed through.

- Ladle into warm bowls, scatter over chopped coriander leaves and serve.

 Spicy Black Bean and Spring Onion Salad Put a 100 g (2½ oz) bag mixed salad leaves, a rinsed and drained 400 g (12 oz) can black beans, 6 sliced spring onions, 2 finely diced red chillies and a small handful of chopped coriander leaves in a large salad bowl. Pour 150 ml (¼ pint) shop-bought fresh French salad dressing and 2 tablespoons sweet chilli sauce over the salad, toss to mix well and serve with warm bread rolls.

Spicy Black Bean, Spring Onion and Noodle Omelette Cook 200 g (7 oz) dried egg noodles according to the packet instructions, then drain and set aside. Meanwhile, heat 2 tablespoons sunflower oil in a medium ovenproof frying pan, add 2 finely diced red chillies, 8 sliced spring onions and 2 finely chopped garlic cloves and cook over a medium heat for 2–4 minutes, then add a rinsed and drained 400 g (12 oz) can black beans. Meanwhile, lightly beat 6 eggs in a bowl and stir in a small handful of chopped coriander leaves and season. Add the drained noodles to the frying pan and stir to mix well. Pour over the egg mixture and cook over a medium heat for 8–10 minutes or until the base is set, then place the pan under a preheated medium-hot grill and cook for 2–4 minutes or until the top is lightly golden and set. Serve warm or at room temperature, cut into wedges.

30 Carrot and Black Bean Curry

Serves 4

500 ml (17 fl oz) vegetable stock, plus extra if needed

4 large carrots, peeled and cut into 1.5 cm (½ inch) dice

400 g (13 oz) can black beans, rinsed and drained

4 plum tomatoes

2 tablespoons sunflower oil

2 teaspoons cumin seeds

1 teaspoon fennel seeds

2 shallots, finely chopped

2 red chillies, finely chopped

1 teaspoon grated fresh root ginger

3 garlic cloves, finely chopped

1 teaspoon ground turmeric

1 teaspoon garam masala

juice of 1 lime

4 tablespoons finely chopped coriander leaves

steamed rice, to serve

- Pour the stock into a saucepan and bring to the boil, add the carrots, reduce the heat and simmer for about 8 minutes or until tender. Stir in the black beans and simmer for a further 2 minutes. Drain and set aside, reserving the stock.

- Meanwhile, put the tomatoes in a heatproof bowl and pour over boiling water to cover. Leave for 5 minutes, then plunge into cold water and drain. Cut a cross at the stem end of each tomato and peel off the skins. Roughly chop, then set aside.

- Heat the oil in a heavy-based saucepan and add the cumin seeds, fennel seeds, shallots, red chillies, ginger and garlic and cook, stirring, over a medium heat for 3–4 minutes until the shallots are softened. Add the tomatoes and 100 ml (3½ fl oz) of the reserved stock, reduce the heat to low and cook, stirring, for about 2 minutes. Stir in the turmeric and cook for a further 2 minutes. Stir in the reserved carrot and beans and simmer for 3–4 minutes, adding more stock if the curry looks dry.

- Remove from the heat and stir in the garam masala, lime juice and coriander. Ladle into warm bowls and serve with steamed rice.

Spicy Carrot and Black Bean Salad

Heat a frying pan until hot, add 2 teaspoons cumin seeds and dry-fry until browned, then remove from the pan and set aside. Put 2 large peeled and coarsely grated carrots and 2 rinsed and drained 400 g (12 oz) cans black beans in a salad bowl. Stir in 1 finely chopped red chilli, the juice of 2 limes and the toasted cumin seeds. Season, then stir in 4 tablespoons finely chopped coriander. Toss to mix, then serve.

Spicy Carrot and Black Bean Noodles

Heat 2 tablespoons sunflower oil in a large wok or frying pan until hot, add 2 finely chopped red chillies, 1 finely chopped onion, 2 chopped garlic cloves and 1 teaspoon peeled and grated fresh root ginger and stir-fry over a medium heat for 4–5 minutes until softened. Add 2 large peeled and coarsely grated carrots and stir-fry for a further 2–4 minutes, then stir in a rinsed and drained 400 g (12 oz) can black beans, 400 g (12 oz) fresh egg noodles and 2 tablespoons oyster sauce. Stir to mix well and heat through until piping hot. Season well and serve immediately.

 # Spicy Smoked Salmon, Pea and Asparagus Pasta

Serves 4

400 g (13 oz) dried bucatini, linguine or spaghetti
200 g (7 oz) asparagus tips, halved lengthways
1 tablespoon butter
1 tablespoon olive oil
1 red chilli, finely chopped
1 teaspoon dried red chilli flakes
2 garlic cloves, finely chopped
2 shallots, finely chopped
200 g (7 oz) crème fraîche
200 g (7 oz) smoked salmon, roughly chopped
100 g (3½ oz) frozen peas
4 tablespoons finely chopped dill
salt and pepper
green salad, to serve

- Cook the pasta in a large saucepan of lightly salted boiling water according to the packet instructions until al dente, adding the asparagus 2 minutes before the end of the cooking time.

- Heat the butter and oil in a large frying pan, add the red chilli, chilli flakes, garlic and shallots and cook over a medium heat for 2–3 minutes.

- Drain the pasta and asparagus, then add to the frying pan with the crème fraiche, smoked salmon, peas and chopped dill and heat through until piping hot, then season.

- Serve in warm bowls with a crisp green salad.

10 Spicy Smoked Salmon, Pea and Asparagus and Pasta Salad

Cook 200 g (10 oz) fresh penne, 100 g (3½ oz) frozen peas and 400 g (12 oz) asparagus tips in a pan of lightly salted boiling water for 2–4 minutes, or according to the pasta packet instructions, until the pasta is al dente. Drain, refresh under cold running water and drain again. Put in a salad bowl with 400 g (12 oz) chopped smoked salmon. Mix together 1 teaspoon dried red chilli flakes, 1 teaspoon medium curry powder and 175 ml (6 fl oz) shop-bought French salad dressing. Pour over the pasta, toss and serve.

30 Spicy Asparagus, Pea and Smoked Salmon Risotto

Heat 2 tablespoons sunflower oil and 2 tablespoons butter in a heavy-based saucepan, add 1 chopped onion, 2 finely chopped red chillies and 2 chopped garlic cloves and cook for 2–3 minutes until beginning to soften. Add 275 g (12 oz) risotto rice and 400 g (12 oz) asparagus tips and stir for 1–2 minutes until the rice is well coated, then add 150 ml (¼ pint) dry white wine and simmer for 1 minute, stirring continuously. Reduce the heat, then add 1.2 litres (2 pints) hot vegetable stock, one ladleful at a time, stirring continuously until each ladleful is absorbed, and cook until the rice is tender but still firm (al dente). Add in 100 g (3½ oz) frozen peas and stir in 200 g (7 oz) roughly chopped smoked salmon, then remove the pan from the heat and stir in 100 g (2½ oz) grated Parmesan cheese and the finely grated rind of 1 lemon. Season well and serve.

30 Harissa Tabbouleh with Roasted Vegetables

Serves 4

1 courgette, cut into bite-
sized pieces

2 red peppers, cored, deseeded
and cut into bite-sized pieces

1 yellow pepper, cored, deseeded
and cut into bite-sized pieces

4 tablespoons olive oil

3 garlic cloves, crushed

1 red chilli, finely chopped

2 tablespoons harissa paste

125 g (4 oz) bulgar wheat

600 ml (1 pint) hot vegetable
stock

juice of 1 lemon

6 tablespoons finely chopped
coriander leaves

6 tablespoons finely chopped
mint leaves

- Put the courgettes and peppers in a roasting tin. Mix together the oil, garlic, red chilli and harissa in a bowl, then pour over the vegetables and toss to coat evenly. Place in a preheated oven, 200°C (400°F), Gas Mark 6, for 20 minutes or until softened and the vegetables are just beginning to char at the edges.

- Meanwhile, put the bulgar wheat in a large heatproof bowl and pour over the stock, then cover tightly with clingfilm and leave to stand for 15 minutes until the grains are tender but still have a little bite.

- Leave the bulgar wheat to cool slightly, then add the roasted vegetables, lemon juice and chopped herbs and toss to mix well. Serve warm or at room temperature.

 Moroccan Vegetable Couscous Salad Put 500 g (1 lb) shop-bought fresh Moroccan-style couscous salad in a large bowl with a 100 g (2½ oz) bag mixed salad leaves, 2 drained 270 g (9 oz) jars chargrilled peppers in olive oil and a small handful each of chopped coriander and mint leaves. Season, then toss to mix well and serve.

 Harissa Vegetable Stew with Bulgar Wheat Put 125 g (4 oz) bulgar wheat in a large heatproof bowl and pour over 600 ml (1 pint) water, then cover tightly with clingfilm and leave to stand for 15 minutes until the grains are tender. Meanwhile, heat 2 tablespoons olive oil in a heavy-based saucepan, add 1 chopped onion, 2 chopped garlic cloves, 2 cored, deseeded and finely chopped red peppers and 1 finely chopped courgette and cook over a medium heat for 1–2 minutes. Add 500 ml (17 fl oz) hot vegetable stock and 1 tablespoon harissa paste and bring to the boil, then reduce the heat and cook for 10–15 minutes or until the vegetables are tender. Season and stir in 2 tablespoons each of finely chopped coriander and mint leaves. Serve with the cooked bulgar wheat.

30 Spicy Roasted Veg Couscous with Cashews and Feta

Serves 4

2 red peppers, cored, deseeded
and cut into 2 cm (¾ inch) pieces
1 yellow pepper, cored, deseeded
and cut into 2 cm (¾ inch) pieces
1 courgette, cut into 2 cm
(¾ inch) cubes
2 large red onions, thickly sliced
4 tablespoons olive oil
200 g (7 oz) couscous
100 g (3½ oz) cashew nuts
handful of chopped mint
handful of chopped coriander
6–8 preserved lemons, halved
200 g (7 oz) feta cheese, crumbled
salt and pepper

For the dressing

juice of 1 orange
5 tablespoons extra-virgin olive oil
1 teaspoon sweet smoked paprika
1 red chilli, finely chopped
1 teaspoon ground cumin
1 teaspoon mild curry powder

- Put the vegetables on a large baking sheet, then drizzle over the oil and season well. Place in a preheated oven, 200°C (400°F), Gas Mark 6, for 12–15 minutes or until softened and the vegetables are just beginning to char at the edges.

- Meanwhile, put the couscous in a large heatproof bowl and season well. Pour over boiling water to just cover, then cover with clingfilm and leave to stand for 8–10 minutes, or according to the packet instructions, until the water is absorbed.

- To make the dressing, mix together all the ingredients in a bowl and season well, then set aside.

- To toast the cashews, heat a frying pan until hot, add the cashews and dry-fry over a medium heat until lightly brown, then remove from the pan and set aside.

- Gently fork the couscous to separate the grains and place in a large, shallow serving dish, then fold in the roasted vegetables, herbs and preserved lemons. Pour the dressing over the couscous and toss to mix well. Scatter with the toasted cashews and feta cheese and serve.

 Spicy Veg, Cashew and Feta Couscous Salad Put 500 g (1 lb) shop-bought fresh spicy vegetable couscous salad in a large bowl with 25 g (1½ oz) each of chopped mint and coriander leaves and 6 sliced spring onions. Add 150 g (5 oz) crumbled feta cheese and 100 g (2½ oz) cashew nuts, toasted as above. Season, then toss to mix well and serve.

 Spicy Veg and Cashew Stew with Feta and Couscous Heat 2 tablespoons olive oil in a heavy-based saucepan, add 2 roughly chopped red onions, 1 finely chopped garlic clove, 2 sliced red chillies, 1 roughly diced courgette, 1 cored, deseeded and diced red pepper and 1 cored, deseeded and diced yellow pepper and cook over a medium heat for 2–4 minutes until softened. Add a 400 g (12 oz) can chopped tomatoes and 200 ml (7 fl oz) hot vegetable stock and bring to a boil, then reduce the heat to medium and cook for 15 minutes or until the vegetables are tender. Season, remove from the heat and stir in 100 g (2½ oz) cashew nuts, toasted as above, and crumble over 100 g (2½ oz) feta cheese. Stir in a small handful each of mint and coriander, then serve with couscous.

HOT-PULS-WON

30 Spicy Pork with Crispy Noodles

Serves 4

sunflower oil, for deep-frying
250 g (8 oz) rice vermicelli
   noodles, broken into pieces
400 g (13 oz) minced pork
3 garlic cloves, finely chopped
2 spring onions, finely chopped,
   plus 2 spring onions,
   finely shredded
3 tablespoons lime juice
2 tablespoons fish sauce
6 tablespoons sweet chilli sauce
1 tablespoon hot chilli sauce
1 tablespoon tomato purée
1 teaspoon dried red chilli flakes
100 g (3½ oz) firm tofu, cut into
   1 cm (½ inch) dice
100 g (3½ oz) coriander leaves
   and stalks, chopped
50 g (2 oz) bean sprouts
2–3 Thai bird's eye chillies,
   finely sliced

- Fill a large wok or deep saucepan one-quarter full with sunflower oil and heat until 180–190°C (350–375°F), or until a cube of bread browns in 30 seconds. Add the noodles, in batches if necessary, and deep-fry in the oil for 30–40 seconds or until they puff up and are lightly golden. Remove with a slotted spoon and drain on kitchen paper.

- Carefully pour all but 2 tablespoons of the oil out of the wok, add the pork and stir-fry over a high heat for 4–5 minutes or until it is browned and cooked through, then transfer to a plate and keep warm.

- Reduce the heat to medium-low, add the garlic and spring onions and stir-fry for 1–2 minutes. Stir in the lime juice, sauces, tomato purée and chilli flakes, reduce the heat to low and simmer for 3–4 minutes or until syrupy. Stir half of the fried rice noodles into the sauce and toss to coat evenly. Stir in the pork and the remaining noodles and heat through.

- Divide the mixture on to large serving plates, top with the tofu, shredded spring onions, chopped coriander, bean sprouts and bird's eye chillies and serve immediately.

---

10 Spicy Pork and Noodle Stir-Fry

Heat 2 tablespoons sunflower oil in a large wok or frying pan until hot, add 1 finely chopped red chilli and 400 g (12 oz) minced pork and stir-fry over a high heat for 1–2 minutes or until browned. Add a 175 g (6 oz) sachet sweet chilli stir-fry sauce and 400 g (12 oz) fresh egg noodles and stir-fry for a further 2–2 minutes or until piping hot and the pork is cooked through. Serve immediately.

20 Spicy Pork and Noodle Omelette

Heat 2 tablespoons sunflower oil in a medium ovenproof frying pan, add 8 sliced spring onions, 2 finely chopped red chillies, 2 chopped garlic cloves and 200 g (7 oz) minced pork and cook over a high heat for 2–4 minutes or until the pork is browned and cooked through. Add 200 g (7 oz) fresh egg noodles and stir to mix well. Meanwhile, whisk together 4 large eggs, 1 tablespoon hot chilli sauce and 2 tablespoons sweet chilli sauce in a bowl, then pour into the pan. Cook for 6–8 minutes until the base is beginning to set, then place the pan under a preheated medium-hot grill and cook for 2–4 minutes or until the top is golden and set. Serve warm or at room temperature, cut into wedges.

 # Spicy Bean and Mixed Pepper Salad

Serves 4

400 g (13 oz) can red kidney beans
400 g (13 oz) can cannellini beans
400 g (13 oz) can butter beans
1 red pepper
1 green pepper
1 yellow pepper
1 small red onion, finely diced
2 red chillies, finely diced
2 celery stalks, finely diced
small handful of chopped
   coriander leaves, to garnish
salt and pepper

For the dressing

6 tablespoons extra-virgin olive oil
juice of 1 large lemon
2 tablespoons cider vinegar
1 teaspoons runny honey

- Rinse and drain the tinned beans and put in a large bowl. Core, deseed and finely dice the peppers, then add to the bowl along with the onion, chillies and celery.

- Mix together all the dressing ingredients in a small bowl. Pour the dressing over the salad, season and toss to mix well.

- Scatter with chopped coriander leaves and serve with toasted ciabatta bread or steamed rice, if liked.

 ### Spicy Bean and Red Pepper Curry

Heat 2 tablespoons olive oil in a large frying pan, add 2 chopped red chillies, 1 chopped red onion, 2 chopped garlic cloves and 2 cored, deseeded and roughly chopped red peppers and cook over a medium heat, stirring, for 4–5 minutes. Stir in 1 tablespoon curry powder and 200 ml (7 fl oz) canned coconut milk and bring to the boil. Add 2 rinsed and drained 410 g (12 oz) cans mixed beans, reduce the heat to medium and cook for 8 minutes. Stir in a handful of chopped coriander and serve.

 ### Spiced Bean and Red Pepper Pilau

Heat 2 tablespoons sunflower oil in a heavy-based saucepan, add 1 chopped onion and cook, stirring, for 1–2 minutes. Stir in 2 teaspoons cumin seeds, 2 sliced red chillies, 1 cinnamon stick, 1 tablespoon mild curry powder, 2 cored, deseeded and diced red peppers and a rinsed and drained 410 g (12 oz) can mixed beans and cook for a further 1–2 minutes, then stir in 250 g (8 oz) basmati rice and 650 ml (1 pint 2 fl oz) hot vegetable stock and bring to the boil. Cover tightly, reduce the heat to low and cook, undisturbed, for 15–20 minutes or until the liquid is absorbed and the rice is tender. Remove from the heat and leave to stand for a few minutes before serving.

HOT-PULS-KYF

30 Spicy Lentil and Carrot Soup with Caramelized Onions

Serves 4

2 tablespoons sunflower oil
1 garlic clove, finely chopped
1 teaspoon grated fresh root ginger
1 red chilli, finely chopped
1 onion, finely chopped
1 tablespoon sweet smoked
   paprika, plus extra to garnish
700 g (1½ lb) carrots, peeled and
   finely chopped
150 g (5 oz) red split lentils,
   rinsed and drained
150 ml (¼ pint) single cream
1 litre (1¾ pints) hot
   vegetable stock
100 ml (3½ fl oz) crème fraîche
small handful of chopped
   coriander leaves
salt and pepper

For the caramelized onions

1 tablespoon butter
1 tablespoon olive oil
1 onion, thinly sliced

- Heat the sunflower oil in a heavy-based saucepan, add the garlic, ginger, red chilli, onion and smoked paprika and cook, stirring, over a medium-high heat for 1–2 minutes. Add the carrots, lentils, cream and stock and bring to the boil, then reduce the heat to medium and simmer, uncovered, for 15–20 minutes.

- Meanwhile, to make the caramelized onions, heat the butter and olive oil in a frying pan, add the onion and cook over a low heat for 12–15 minutes or until caramelized and golden brown. Drain on kitchen paper and keep warm.

- Using an electric stick blender, blend the lentil mixture in the pan until smooth, then season well.

- Ladle into bowls, add a dollop of crème fraiche and scatter with chopped coriander leaves and the caramelized onions. Sprinkle with a little smoked paprika before serving.

---

10 Spicy Lentil and Carrot Salad

Put 2 rinsed and drained 400 g (12 oz) cans green lentils, 2 peeled and coarsely grated carrots, 1 finely chopped red chilli, 4 sliced spring onions and a large handful of chopped coriander leaves in a salad bowl. Pour 150 ml (¼ pint) shop-bought fresh French salad dressing over the salad and add 1 teaspoon sweet smoked paprika. Season, toss to mix and serve.

20 Spicy Lentil and Carrot Dhal

Put 150 g (5 oz) rinsed and drained red split lentils, 2 peeled and finely diced carrots, 1 chopped onion, 2 teaspoons peeled and grated fresh root ginger, 2 teaspoons grated garlic, 2 teaspoons cumin seeds, 2 teaspoons black mustard seeds and 1 tablespoon medium or hot curry powder in a saucepan, then pour in 800 ml (1 pint 8 fl oz) hot vegetable stock and bring to a boil. Reduce the heat to medium and cook, uncovered, for 12–15 minutes or until thickened and the lentils are just tender. Season, stir in a small handful of chopped coriander leaves and serve with steamed rice or bread.

HOT-PULS-KEG

 # Singapore Rice Noodles

Serves 4

250 g (8 oz) dried rice noodles
4 tablespoons vegetable oil
500 g (1 lb) raw peeled
    tiger prawns
100 g (3½ oz) bacon lardons
3 garlic cloves, crushed
1 red chilli, thinly sliced, plus extra
    to garnish
1 teaspoon grated fresh root ginger
1 onion, thinly sliced
1 large carrot, peeled and cut into
    thin sticks
200 g (7 oz) sugarsnap peas,
    thinly sliced
50 g (2 oz) bean sprouts
6 spring onions, finely sliced
    diagonally
1–2 tablespoons medium or hot
    curry powder
2 tablespoons water
6 tablespoons dark soy sauce
pepper
lime wedges, to serve

- Cook the noodles following the packet instructions, then drain and set aside.

- Heat 2 tablespoons of the oil in a large wok or frying pan until hot, add the prawns and lardons and stir-fry over a high heat for 4–5 minutes or until the prawns turn pink and the bacon is lightly golden. Use a slotted spoon to transfer the prawns and bacon to a plate and keep warm. Rinse out the wok or pan and wipe dry with kitchen paper.

- Heat the remaining oil in the wok or pan until hot, add the garlic, red chilli and ginger and stir-fry over a high heat for 30 seconds or until lightly browned, then add the onion and vegetables and stir-fry for a further 3–4 minutes until just beginning to soften, then add the curry powder and continue to stir for a further 1 minute.

- Add the drained noodles and measurement water and toss well, then stir in the soy sauce, season with pepper and stir-fry for 1 minute. Toss the prawns and bacon through the mixture and heat through until piping hot.

- Divide the noodles into warm shallow bowls or plates, scatter with extra sliced red chillies and serve with lime wedges to squeeze over.

 Spicy Rice Noodle Soup

Put 200 g (10 oz) fresh rice noodles, 1 tablespoon tom yum paste and 800 ml (1 pint 8 fl oz) hot vegetable stock in a saucepan and bring to the boil, then cook for 2–2 minutes. Stir in 400 g (12 oz) cooked peeled prawns and cook for a further 1 minute or until piping hot. Serve immediately.

Spicy Rice Noodle Omelette

Whisk together 6 eggs, 6 finely sliced spring onions and 1 tablespoon medium or hot curry powder in a bowl, then season well. Heat 2 tablespoons olive oil in a large ovenproof frying pan, add 250 g (8 oz) raw peeled tiger prawns and stir-fry over a high heat for 4–5 minutes or until the prawns turn pink, then add

200 g (10 oz) fresh rice noodles and pour over the egg mixture. Cook over a medium heat for 10–12 minutes or until the base is set, then place the pan under a preheated medium-hot grill and cook for 4–5 minutes or until the top is golden and set. Leave to cool, then serve cut into wedges with a green salad.

Puy Lentil and Butter Bean Salad with Chilli Dressing

Serves 4

400 g (13 oz) can Puy lentils, rinsed and drained

400 g (13 oz) can butter beans, rinsed and drained

1 red onion, finely sliced

200 g (7 oz) cherry tomatoes, halved

50 g (2 oz) flat leaf parsley, roughly chopped

For the dressing

6 tablespoons extra-virgin olive oil

2 red chillies, very finely diced

2 tablespoons red wine vinegar

1 teaspoon Dijon or wholegrain mustard

1 teaspoon runny honey

½ garlic clove, crushed

- Put the lentils and butter beans in a large serving bowl, then add the onion, cherry tomatoes and parsley.

- Mix together all the dressing ingredients in a small bowl, then pour over the salad, toss to mix well and serve.

---

2 **Puy Lentil and Butter Bean Pilau with Chilli Dressing** Cook 250 g (11½ oz) basmati rice in a large saucepan of lightly salted boiling water according to the packet instructions. Meanwhile, make the Puy Lentil and Butter Bean Salad with Chilli Dressing as above. Drain the rice, then stir into the lentil salad and toss to mix well. Serve warm or at room temperature.

3 **Chillied Puy Lentil and Butter Bean Pasta** Cook 250 g (11½ oz) orzo pasta in a large saucepan of lightly salted boiling water according to the packet instructions until just al dente, then drain and return to the pan. Cover and keep warm. Heat 2 tablespoons sunflower oil in a large frying pan, add 1 sliced red onion, 2 sliced red chillies and 2 sliced garlic cloves and cook over a medium heat, stirring occasionally, for 5–6 minutes until softened. Stir in a rinsed and drained 400 g (12 oz) can Puy lentils, a rinsed and drained 400 g (12 oz) can butter beans, 175 ml (6 fl oz) hot vegetable stock and the cooked orzo and bring to the boil, then reduce the heat to medium, cover and cook for 5–6 minutes, stirring occasionally. Season, then stir in a small handful of chopped flat leaf parsley and serve.

20 Spiced Prawn, Coconut and Banh Pho Pot

Serves 4

1 tablespoon sunflower oil
6 pink shallots, finely sliced
1 red chilli, finely sliced, plus extra
   slivers to garnish
1 green chilli, finely sliced
1 cinnamon stick
1 star anise
5 cm (2 inch) piece of fresh root
   ginger, peeled and thinly sliced
8 cm (3 inch) length of trimmed
   lemon grass stalk, finely chopped
400 ml (14 fl oz) hot fish stock
2 tablespoons fish sauce
1 tablespoon soft brown sugar
400 g (13 oz) raw peeled tiger
   prawns
6 baby pak choi, halved or quartered
400 ml (14 fl oz) can coconut milk
juice of 2 limes
250 g (8 oz) dried flat rice
   noodles (banh pho)
sliced spring onions, to garnish

- Heat the oil in a saucepan, add the shallots, chillies, cinnamon stick, star anise and ginger and cook gently for 2 minutes. Add the lemon grass and stock and bring to a simmer.

- Stir in the fish sauce, sugar and prawns and simmer for 5–6 minutes or until the prawns turn pink and are cooked through. Add the pak choi, coconut milk and lime juice and heat through until the pak choi wilts.

- Cook the noodles according to the packet instructions, then drain. Divide the noodles into warm bowls and ladle over the pho mixture. Scatter with slivered red chillies and spring onions and serve immediately.

 Spicy Prawn and Coconut Noodle Soup Put 600 ml (1 pint) hot vegetable stock, 1 tablespoon medium curry paste and a 400 ml (14 fl oz) can coconut milk and in a saucepan and bring to the boil. Add 200 g (10 oz) fresh rice noodles and 400 g (12 oz) cooked peeled prawns and cook for 1–2 minutes or until piping hot. Remove from the heat and squeeze over the juice of 1 lime. Serve immediately.

Spicy Coconut Prawns with Angel-Hair Pasta Cook 400 g (12 oz) angel-hair pasta in a large saucepan of lightly salted boiling water according to the packet instructions. Heat 1 tablespoon sunflower oil in a heavy-based saucepan, add 1 chopped onion, 2 chopped red chillies and 2 chopped garlic cloves and cook over a low heat, stirring occasionally, for 6–8 minutes until softened. Add 500 g (1 lb) raw peeled tiger prawns to the onions, increase the heat to medium and cook for 5–6 minutes or until they turn pink and are cooked through. Stir in 200 ml (7 fl oz) coconut cream and a small handful each of chopped coriander and Thai basil leaves. Drain the pasta, then add to the prawn mixture. Season, toss to mix well and serve immediately.

HOT-PULS-QEQ

Spicy Tuna, Tomato and Olive Pasta

Serves 4

350 g (11½ oz) dried penne
2 x 400 g (13 oz) cans tuna
   chunks in water, drained
2 red chillies, finely chopped
1 teaspoon dried red chilli flakes
200 g (7 oz) pitted black olives
240 g (8 oz) tub sun-blushed
   tomatoes in oil
salt and pepper
chopped flat leaf parsley,
   to garnish

- Cook the pasta in a large saucepan of lightly salted boiling water according to the packet instructions until al dente.

- Meanwhile, put the tuna in a large bowl and roughly flake with a fork, then add the red chillies, chilli flakes, olives and tomatoes with their oil.

- Drain the pasta, add to the tuna mixture and toss to mix well, then season.

- Spoon into warm bowls, scatter with chopped parsley and serve.

 Spicy Tuna, Tomato and Olive Pasta

Salad Cook 200 g (10 oz) fresh penne in a large saucepan of lightly salted boiling water for 2–4 minutes, or according to the packet instructions, until al dente. Drain, then refresh under cold running water and drain again. Meanwhile, put 2 drained 400 g (12 oz) cans tuna in water in a salad bowl and roughly flake with a fork, then add 200 g (7 oz) pitted black olives, 2 roughly chopped plum tomatoes, 1 finely chopped red chilli and a small handful of chopped flat leaf parsley. Add the drained pasta, then drizzle over 1 tablespoon chilli oil and 2 tablespoons extra-virgin olive oil and squeeze over the juice of 1 lemon. Season, toss to mix well and serve.

Spicy Tuna, Tomato and Olive Pasta

Bake Cook 250 g (11½ oz) dried fusilli in a large saucepan of lightly salted boiling water according to the packet instructions until al dente. Meanwhile, heat 2 tablespoons olive oil in a large frying pan, add 200 g (7 oz) halved small button mushrooms, 2 finely chopped red chillies and 1 sliced bunch of spring onions and cook over a medium heat for 5 minutes or until softened. Stir in 200 g (7 oz) cream cheese with garlic and herbs, 4 tablespoons double cream, 200 g (7 oz) halved cherry tomatoes and 200 g (7 oz) pitted black olives and gently heat through, stirring occasionally, until the cream cheese and cream have combined to make a sauce. Drain and flake a 400 g (12 oz) can tuna in water. Drain the pasta, then mix with the tuna and creamy sauce. Transfer to an ovenproof dish and sprinkle with 75 g (2 oz) grated mature Cheddar cheese. Place in a preheated oven, 180°C (350°F), Gas Mark 4, for 10 minutes or until lightly browned. Serve immediately with a green salad.

30 Spiced Rice and Yellow Lentils

Serves 4

3 tablespoons sunflower oil

1 onion, finely chopped

4 tablespoons shop-bought
crispy onions

1 teaspoon ground turmeric

1 tablespoon cumin seeds

1 dried red chilli

1 cinnamon stick

3 whole cloves

½ teaspoon crushed
cardamom seeds

225 g (7½ oz) basmati rice

125 g (4 oz) yellow split lentils,
rinsed and drained

600 ml (1 pint) hot vegetable stock

6 tablespoons finely chopped
coriander leaves

salt and pepper

To serve (optional)

pickles

poppadums

natural yogurt

- Heat the oil in a heavy-based saucepan, add the onion and crispy onions and cook over a medium heat for 1–2 minutes, then add the spices and cook for a further 2–3 minutes until fragrant. Add the rice and lentils and stir to coat well for 1–2 minutes.

- Pour in the stock, add the coriander and season well. Bring to the boil, then reduce the heat to low, cover tightly and cook for 10 minutes. Remove from the heat and leave to stand, covered, for 10 minutes.

- Spoon into bowls and serve with pickles, poppadums and yogurt, if liked.

 Spicy Rice and Lentil Soup

Put 2 x 400 g (12 oz) cans lentil soup, 2 teaspoons mild curry paste and 200 g (7 oz) shop-bought ready-cooked basmati rice in a saucepan and bring to the boil, then reduce the heat to medium and cook for 2–4 minutes or until piping hot. Serve with dollops of yogurt and warm crusty bread.

 Spicy Vegetable and Lentil Stew

Heat 2 tablespoons sunflower oil in a saucepan, add 1 chopped onion, 2 teaspoons peeled and grated fresh root ginger, 2 teaspoons grated garlic, 2 finely chopped red chillies and 1 tablespoon medium curry paste and cook for 2–3 minutes, then stir in 2 x 400 g (12 oz) cans lentil soup and 500 g (1 lb) frozen mixed vegetables. Bring to the boil, then reduce the heat to medium-low and cook for 6–8 minutes or until piping hot. Serve with crusty bread or steamed rice.

HOT-PULS-BOH

30 Spicy Prawn and Pea Pilau

Serves 4

1 tablespoon sunflower oil
1 tablespoon butter
1 large onion, finely chopped
2 garlic cloves, finely chopped
1 tablespoon medium or hot
 curry paste
250 g (8 oz) basmati rice
600 ml (1 pint) hot fish or
 vegetable stock
300 g (10 oz) frozen peas
finely grated rind and juice
 of 1 large lime
20 g (¾ oz) coriander,
 finely chopped
400 g (13 oz) cooked
 peeled prawns
salt and pepper

· Heat the oil and butter in a heavy-based saucepan, add the onion and cook over a medium heat for 2–3 minutes until softened. Stir in the garlic and curry paste and cook for a further 1–2 minutes until fragrant, then add the rice and stir to coat well.

· Stir in the stock, peas and lime rind, then season well and bring to the boil. Cover tightly, then reduce the heat to low and cook for 12–15 minutes or until the liquid is absorbed and the rice is tender.

· Remove the pan from the heat, then stir in the lime juice, coriander and prawns. Cover and leave the prawns to heat through for a few minutes before serving.

 Spicy Prawn and Pea Stir-Fried Rice

Heat 2 tablespoons sunflower oil in a large wok or frying pan until hot, add 1 tablespoon medium curry paste, 400 g (12 oz) cooked peeled prawns, 200 g (7 oz) frozen peas and 500 g (1 lb) shop-bought ready-cooked basmati rice and stir-fry over a high heat for 4–5 minutes or until piping hot. Remove from the heat, season and stir in 6 tablespoons chopped coriander leaves. Serve immediately.

 Spicy Prawn, Pea and Rice Soup

Heat 1 tablespoon butter in a saucepan, add 1 tablespoon mild curry powder and stir for 20–40 seconds, then add 6 sliced spring onions, 1 chopped garlic clove and 1 teaspoon peeled and grated fresh root ginger and cook for a further 1–2 minutes. Pour in 800 ml (1 pint 8 fl oz) hot fish stock and bring to the boil, then cook, uncovered, for 4–5 minutes. Add 400 g (12 oz) raw peeled tiger prawns, 200 g (7 oz) frozen peas and 100 g (2½ oz) shop-bought ready-cooked basmati rice. Bring back to the boil, then reduce the heat to medium and cook for 5–6 minutes until the prawns turn pink and the rice and peas are tender. Season and remove from the heat, then stir in 4 tablespoons finely chopped coriander leaves and serve.

30 Spiced Broad Bean and Dill Pilau

Serves 4

250 g (8 oz) basmati rice
300 g (10 oz) podded
  broad beans
50 g (2 oz) butter
2 red chillies, finely chopped
1 tablespoon cumin seeds
2 cloves
6 green cardamom pods
1 cinnamon stick
50 g (2 oz) red split lentils, rinsed
  and drained
6 finely sliced spring onions
6 tablespoons finely chopped dill
salt and pepper

- Cook the broad beans in a saucepan of boiling water for 1–2 minutes. Drain, then put in a bowl of cold water and leave the beans to cool slightly. Drain again, then slip off and discard the skins and set the beans aside.

- Melt the butter in a saucepan over a low heat, add the red chillies and spices and stir for 1 minute, then add the lentils and rice and continue to stir until well coated.

- Pour over enough water to come about 1.5 cm (¾ inch) above the level of the rice. Season well and bring to the boil. Stir once, then reduce the heat to very low, cover tightly and cook gently for 8–10 minutes. Remove from the heat and leave to stand, covered, for 10–12 minutes or until the liquid is absorbed and the rice is tender.

- Stir the broad beans, spring onions and dill through the rice, then spoon into a bowls and serve.

 Spicy Broad Bean and Dill Rice Salad

Blanch and skin 400 g (12 oz) podded broad beans as above. Meanwhile, heat a frying pan until hot, add 1 tablespoon cumin seeds and dry-fry over a medium heat until browned, then leave to cool. Put 500 g (1 lb) shop-bought fresh boiled rice, 2 finely chopped red chillies, the toasted cumin seeds, 6 finely sliced spring onions and the broad beans in a large bowl. Pour 150 ml (¼ pint) shop-bought fresh vinaigrette over the salad and scatter with a small handful of chopped dill. Season, toss to mix well and serve.

 Spicy Broad Bean and Dill Pasta

Cook 275 g (12 oz) dried penne in a large saucepan of lightly salted boiling water according to the packet instructions until al dente, adding 200 g (10 oz) podded broad beans 2–4 minutes before the end of the cooking time. Meanwhile, heat 1 tablespoon butter in a large frying pan, add 6 finely sliced spring onions, 2 finely chopped red chillies and 2 finely chopped garlic cloves and cook over a low heat for 2–4 minutes until softened. Add 250 ml (8 fl oz) crème fraîche and heat through for a few minutes until piping hot. Drain the pasta and broad beans, return to the pan and stir in the crème fraiche mixture. Season, toss to mix well and scatter over a small handful of chopped dill before serving.

30 Chilli and Courgette Pennette

Serves 4

1 tablespoon butter
1 tablespoon olive oil
2 red chillies, finely chopped
2 garlic cloves, finely chopped
4 spring onions, very
    finely chopped
3 courgettes, coarsely grated
finely grated rind of 1 lime
150 g (5 oz) cream cheese
350 g (11½ oz) dried pennette or
    other short-shaped pasta
small handful of flat leaf parsley,
    chopped
salt and pepper

- Heat the butter and oil in a large frying pan, add the red chillies, garlic, spring onions and courgettes and cook over a medium–low heat for 10 minutes or until softened.

- Reduce the heat to low, add the lime rind and gently cook for 3–4 minutes, then add the cream cheese and mix together until the cheese melts. Season to taste.

- Meanwhile, cook the pasta in a large saucepan of lightly salted boiling water according to the packet instructions until al dente.

- Drain the pasta and stir into the courgette mixture with the parsley. Spoon into warm bowls and serve.

10 Chilli and Courgette Stir-Fry Noodles

Heat 2 tablespoons olive oil in a large frying pan, add 6 sliced spring onions, 2 crushed garlic cloves, 1 chopped red chilli and 2 coarsely grated courgettes and cook over a high heat for 4–5 minutes until softened, then add 600 g (1 lb 5 oz) fresh egg noodles and 4 tablespoons light soy sauce and toss to mix well. Stir-fry for 1–2 minutes or until piping hot. Serve immediately.

20 Courgette and Chilli Pasta Salad

Cook 250 g (12 oz) dried pennette in a large saucepan of lightly salted boiling water according to the packet instructions until al dente. Drain the pasta, rinse under cold running water and drain again, then leave to cool for 10 minutes. Put 2 coarsely grated courgettes, 4 sliced spring onions, 4 tablespoons each of roughly chopped coriander and mint leaves and 200 g (7 oz) halved cherry tomatoes in a large salad bowl, then add the cooled pasta. Whisk together 2 finely chopped red chillies, 2 crushed garlic cloves, 6 tablespoons extra-virgin olive oil, the juice of 1 lemon and 1 teaspoon honey in a bowl, then season well. Pour the dressing over the salad, toss to mix well and serve.

30 Chilli and Butternut Squash Risotto

Serves 4

50 g (2 oz) butter
1 tablespoon olive oil
1 onion, very finely chopped
2 garlic cloves, finely chopped
2 red chillies, finely chopped
250 g (8 oz) butternut squash
  flesh, cut into small dice
275 g (9 oz) risotto rice,
  such as vialone nano,
  carnaroli or arborio
1 litre (1¾ pints) hot vegetable
  stock
100 g (3½ oz) finely grated
  Parmesan cheese, plus extra
  to serve
salt and pepper
chopped flat leaf parsley,
  to garnish

- Heat the butter and oil in a medium saucepan, add the onion, garlic, red chillies and butternut squash and cook over a medium heat for 3–4 minutes until softened. Add the rice and stir for 1 minute or until the grains are well coated.

- Add 1 ladle of hot stock and simmer, stirring until it has been absorbed. Repeat with another ladle of stock, then continue to add the stock at intervals and cook as before, for a further 18–20 minutes or until the liquid has been absorbed and the rice is tender but still firm (al dente). Reserve 1 ladle of stock.

- When cooked, stir in the reserved stock and Parmesan, season and mix well. Remove from the heat, cover and leave to stand for 2 minutes.

- Spoon into warm bowls, scatter with chopped parsley and serve with extra grated Parmesan.

 Chilli, Butternut Squash and Rice Broth Heat 1 tablespoon butter in a saucepan, add 1 chopped red chilli and cook, stirring, for 1 minute, then add 2 x 400 g (12 oz) cans of root vegetable and butternut squash soup and 200 g (7 oz) shop-bought ready-cooked white rice and bring to the boil. Reduce the heat to medium and cook gently for 2–4 minutes or until piping hot. Serve immediately.

 Butternut Squash and Chilli Pasta Cook 400 g (12 oz) butternut squash flesh, cut into 1 cm (½ inch) cubes, in a large saucepan of lightly salted boiling water for 10 minutes, then add 250 g (11½ oz) quick-cook spaghetti and cook for a further 5 minutes or according to packet instructions, until the squash is tender and the pasta is al dente. Drain well, then return to the saucepan and add 2 tablespoons chilli oil and 100 g (2½ oz) grated Parmesan cheese. Toss to mix well, spoon into warm bowls, scatter with a small handful of chopped flat-leaf parsley and serve.

30 Spicy Chickpea Curry

Serves 4

2 tablespoons sunflower oil
4 garlic cloves, minced
2 teaspoons peeled and finely
   grated fresh root ginger
1 large onion, coarsely grated
1–2 green chillies, finely sliced
1 teaspoon hot chilli powder
1 tablespoon ground cumin
1 tablespoon ground coriander
3 tablespoons natural yogurt,
   plus extra, whisked, to serve
2 teaspoons garam masala
500 ml (17 fl oz) water
2 teaspoons tamarind paste
2 teaspoons medium or hot
   curry powder
2 x 400 g (13 oz) cans chickpeas,
   rinsed and drained
chopped coriander leaves, to
   garnish
lemon wedges, to serve
   (optional)

- Heat the oil in a large heavy-based frying pan, add the garlic, ginger, onion and green chillies and cook over a medium heat, stirring occasionally, for 5–6 minutes until the onion is lightly golden. Add the chilli powder, cumin, ground coriander, yogurt and garam masala and cook for a further 1–2 minutes.

- Stir in the measurement water and bring to the boil. Add the tamarind paste, curry powder and chickpeas and bring back to the boil, then reduce the heat to medium and cook, uncovered, for 15–20 minutes or until the sauce is thickened.

- Ladle into warm bowls, drizzle with extra whisked yogurt and scatter with chopped coriander. Serve with lemon wedges for squeezing over, if liked.

---

10 Spicy Hummus

Put 2 rinsed and drained 400 g (12 oz) cans chickpeas, 1 tablespoon medium or hot curry powder, 1 teaspoon garlic paste, the juice of 1 lemon and 400 g (12 oz) half-fat crème fraîche in a food processor or blender, then season and blend until fairly smooth. Serve with toasted pitta bread and a chopped salad.

20 Spicy Chickpea Soup

Heat 2 tablespoons sunflower oil in a saucepan, add 1 chopped onion and cook, stirring, for 1–2 minutes until softened. Add 1 tablespoon medium or hot curry powder and 600 ml (1 pint) hot vegetable stock and bring to the boil, then add a rinsed and drained 400 g (12 oz) can chickpeas and 200 ml (7 fl oz)

single cream. Bring back to the boil, then reduce the heat to medium and cook for 4–5 minutes or until piping hot. Season, stir in 4 tablespoons chopped coriander leaves and serve with crusty bread.

30 Burmese Coconut Chicken and Rice Noodle Curry

Serves 4

800 g (1¾ lb) boneless, skinless
  chicken thighs, cut into
  bite-sized pieces
2 large onions, roughly chopped
5 garlic cloves, roughly chopped
1 teaspoon peeled and finely
  grated fresh root ginger
2 tablespoons sunflower oil
½ teaspoon Burmese shrimp paste
400 ml (14 fl oz) can coconut milk
2 tablespoons hot curry powder
200 g (7 oz) dried flat rice noodles
salt and pepper
lime wedges, to serve

To garnish

chopped coriander leaves
finely chopped red onion
fried garlic slivers
sliced red chillies

- Season the chicken pieces and set aside. Put the onion, garlic and ginger in a food processor or blender and blend to a smooth paste, adding a little water if needed.

- Heat the oil in a large saucepan, add the onion mixture and shrimp paste and cook, stirring, over a high heat for 4–5 minutes. Add the chicken, reduce the heat to medium and cook, stirring, for 1–2 minutes until browned.

- Stir in the coconut milk and curry powder and bring to the boil, then cover, reduce the heat and simmer for 15–20 minutes, stirring occasionally.

- Meanwhile, cook the noodles according to the packet instructions, then drain and divide into large warm bowls.

- Ladle over the curry, scatter with chopped coriander, chopped red onion, fried garlic slivers and sliced red chillies and serve with lime wedges to squeeze over.

---

10 Spicy Coconut Chicken and Rice Noodles

Heat 2 tablespoons sunflower oil in a large wok until hot, add 8 chopped spring onions, 2 chopped garlic cloves and 1 tablespoon hot curry powder and stir-fry over a high heat for 1–2 minutes. Stir in 275 g (12 oz) fresh rice noodles, 600 g (1 lb 5 oz) shop-bought ready-cooked skinless chicken breasts and 200 ml (7 fl oz) canned coconut milk and stir-fry for a further 1–2 minutes or until piping hot. Serve immediately with lime wedges.

20 Grilled Coconut Chicken with Spicy Rice Noodles

Mix together 2 tablespoons medium or hot curry powder, 100 ml (2½ fl oz) coconut cream and the juice of 1 lime in a small bowl, then brush over 4 large boneless, skin-on chicken breasts. Cook under a preheated medium grill for 6–8 minutes on each side or until cooked through. Meanwhile, put 400 g (12 oz) dried rice noodles in a heatproof bowl, cover with boiling water and leave to stand for 10 minutes, then drain. Put the noodles in a bowl, then add 2 tablespoons extra-virgin olive oil, the juice of 1 lime and 1 finely chopped red chilli, season and toss to mix well. Divide the noodles on to warm plates, top with the grilled chicken and serve immediately.

30 Spicy Quinoa, Broad Bean and Avocado Salad

Serves 4

200 g (7 oz) quinoa

800 ml (1 pint 8 fl oz) hot vegetable stock

500 g (1 lb) podded broad beans

1 tablespoon cumin seeds

3 lemons

2 ripe avocados

2 garlic cloves, crushed

2 red chillies, finely chopped

200 g (7 oz) radishes, thickly sliced

small handful of chopped coriander leaves

5 tablespoons extra-virgin olive oil

salt and pepper

- Put the quinoa in a sieve and rinse well, then put in a medium saucepan and add the stock. Bring to the boil, then reduce the heat to medium and simmer for 10–12 minutes, uncovered, until the germ separates and most of the stock has been absorbed. Drain well, then leave to cool.

- Meanwhile, cook the broad beans in a saucepan of boiling water for 1–2 minutes. Drain, then put in a bowl of cold water and leave the beans to cool slightly. Drain again, then slip off and discard the skins and set the beans aside.

- Heat a frying pan until hot, add the cumin seeds and dry-fry over a medium heat until lightly brown, then remove from the pan and set aside. When cooled, lightly crush the seeds.

- Remove the peel and pith from the lemons and cut each one into segments, discarding any seeds, then put into a large bowl. Squeeze any remaining juices into the bowl.

- Peel, stone and thickly slice the avocados, add to the bowl and toss in the lemon juice. Add the drained quinoa, broad beans, toasted cumin seeds and the remaining ingredients, then season. Toss to mix well and serve.

 Spicy Avocado and Broad Bean Bruschettas Blanch and skin 100 g (2½ oz) podded broad beans as above. Peel, stone and chop 2 avocados, then put in a blender with the skinned broad beans, 2 chopped red chillies, 4 tablespoons chopped flat leaf parsley, 4 tablespoons olive oil and the juice of 1 lemon. Season, then blend until fairly smooth. Spread on to toasted ciabatta slices and serve, drizzled with a little extra olive oil.

 Spicy Quinoa and Broad Bean Broth Put 75 g (2 oz) quinoa and 600 ml (1 pint) water in a saucepan and bring to the boil, then reduce the heat to medium and simmer, uncovered, for 8–10 minutes until the germ separates and most of the liquid has been absorbed. Drain well, then return to the saucepan and add 800 ml (1 pint 8 fl oz) hot vegetable stock, 400 g (12 oz) podded broad beans, 1 tablespoon chilli oil and 1 tablespoon hot curry powder. Season, then bring to the boil, stirring frequently, and cook for 2–4 minutes or until piping hot. Remove from the heat, stir in a small handful of chopped coriander leaves and serve.

Index

Page references in *italics* indicate photographs.

Acknowledgements

Executive editor: Eleanor Maxfield
Editor: Joanne Wilson
Copy-editor: Jo Murray
Art Director: Jonathan Christie
Design: www.gradedesign.com
Art Direction: Juliette Norsworthy & Tracy Killick
Photographer: Craig Robertson
Home economist: Emma Lewis
Stylist: Isabel De Cordova
Production: Peter Hunt